mama RED's
COMFORT KITCHEN
recipes from monday nights at simply red

By: Chef Samantha Izzo

Keep cooking with comfort - Simply Sam '08

SIDE ORDER BOOKS
www.sideorderbooks.com

Published by
Side Order Books
www.sideorderbooks.com

Copyright © May 2008 Side Order Books

Illustrations and font design by Christopher Wolff
Cover design by Joe Lamarre, Art and Anthropology, Inc.
Book design by Anne Kiley

Izzo, Samantha
Mama Red's Comfort Kitchen/Samantha Izzo
ISBN 978-0-9787368-2-8

Printed in the United States of America
First printing, 2008

This book is dedicated to everyone
who makes Simply Red the family that it is.
I love you all and without you none of this
would have been possible.

Acknowledgments

As with all major (and minor) undertakings, one needs to thank those who supported and contributed to the project at hand.

My roots run deep to the South African soil where I was born, and I acknowledge all the love and support I've received in my life.

To my mom for giving me my first cookbooks and eating all of my early creations; to my husband Gary for supplying continual support and love (and the credit line that started the first Simply Red); my daughter Madi who loves to steal the brown sugar cubes from the server station; my maternal Grandmother and Grandfather Willie and Arthur Trigg for all the years of adventure, fun and the gift of my first apron; my paternal grandmother and grandfather Myffy and Granddog Buyskes for all the great meals and days by the coast; my Godparents Liz and Duncan Hindle for teaching me to make tea and helping me stay organized; my brother Dylan--I love your creativety, dedication and support; my sister Kadi--I hope your art work always graces the walls of my restaurant.

To Naureen, Aimee, Jenn, Rebecca and the Hellers, the first friends I made when I moved to this country: I am blessed to have you in my life. My thanks to Richie and friends for the years of amazing music, laughter and tears: it's because of you that I wrote this book. Without you guys there would never have been a Southern night. Here's to our names in lights: Evil City String Band and Mama Red... watch out world!

Thanks to my hardworking staff who scrubbed away all the grease of the old diner and gave me hours, days and weeks of undying dedication. Melissa, thank you for the years that you have given me how we have grown together.

I am grateful to Rose, Roman, Anna and Rachel for clean windows, babysitting Madi, beautiful flowers and never ending support; to Dewi and Rick for being best friends and great business advisors--I hope we grow old together; to Nikki Neufeld and Brian Harper, Madi's godparents for Nantucket, wine, laughter, tears and friendship; to Jim and

Tracey Greene, Caryn and Cole Sheckler, Dana and Shannon, Maria and Doug--I love you guys; and to Emily for caring for and loving Madi.

Thank you to the community of Trumansburg. You've made every Monday night a success. Through power outs and snow storms, we licked our fingers clean! Thank you for embracing our family and for giving us a place to call home.

Chris Wolff, thank you for your incredible illustrations and for putting my recipes into "Mudville"; thanks to Peggy Haine and Peter Hoover for dilly beans; to Jose Gregoria Hernandez for your beautiful words; to Joe Lamarre, an amazing designer, for the book cover and the direction you have taken the restaurant; to Lisa Delaney for the image that is Simply Red; and to Amelia and Leah of Felicia's Atomic Lounge for the creative drink recipes and for your expertise behind the bar.

A special note of appreciation to Chuck Tauck and Bob Madill for giving me and Simply Red a home and room to grow, and to the staff at Sheldrake for accepting the Simply Red family.

Finally, thanks to Michael and Thomas and the creative team at Side Order Books who shared their talents and enthusiasm in the development and production of this book.

Chef Samantha
"Mama Red"

Table of Contents

Foreword .... page - 1

Introduction 3

The Recipes

Beverages	7
From the Pantry	17
Breads	25
Sauces/Butters	37
Salads	47
Appetizers	61
Side Dishes	71
Classic Recipes	85
Specialties	97
Desserts	107
Recipe Index	123
Measurement Conversion Tables	132

About the Winery 57

About the Band 119

Foreword

"Hey Good-Lookin'

Whatcha Got Cookin'?"

With the blues playing on the sound system, a fetching young woman who seemed barely out of her teens, with bright red hair, warbled along while her sauté pans and cooking utensils clanked an arrhythmic tattoo. Lunchtime hunger and curiosity had urged us into the former coffee shop and hub of village news (and gossip) to check out the sequel. One spoonful of Sam's signature chili--rich, vegetarian, and spiked with local beer--and we were hooked.

"Simply Red," the creation of South African-born Samantha Buyskes, with enthusiastic support from her artist husband-to-be, Gary Izzo, was to become our Monday night church-equivalent, a place to find community along with the crispiest fried chicken north of Arkansas, the falling-off-the-bones-iest ribs, and the richest bleu-laced macaroni and cheese bar none. We loved Sam's Killer Shrimp, her rich molasses cake, the soft sweet potato fries dipped in curried mayo, and crisp fried green tomatoes--and that was just the Monday night menu, fixed to go along with transformative Southern string band music played by the locals, many of them nationally recognized: banjo player Richie Stearns, banjo-uke player and vocalist Jim Riedy, and fiddler John Hoffman among them; and whichever itinerant musicians happened through. On Mondays it was reservations only--how many other restaurants can draw an SRO crowd on a Monday night?

The rest of the week's menu was foodie heaven: slow-roasted lamb-shank, Moroccan chicken with preserved lemon, gumbo, sea bass, all served with fresh locally harvested vegetables, and paired with both South African and our fabulous Finger Lakes wines. Heavenly desserts included a blackberry-and-peach cobbler we still dream about. Sam, whose well-trained young staff was exceptionally loyal to her and professional in every way, frequently stepped out of the kitchen to schmooze with the clientele, and all was right with the world.

In 2006 the news was dismal--the Main Street building had been sold, Sam was out of a kitchen, the Monday night mob was out of a place to gather, and the village was bereft of a damned good eatery. While we wallowed in fried-chicken withdrawal, Sheldrake Point Winery's Chuck Tauck and Bob Madill threw us a rope. Knowing a good thing when they saw it, they built a comfy dinner spot for Sam at the winery; it has become a thriving operation, and a delightful place to enjoy estate-grown riesling, beautiful perennial gardens, a spectacular view of Cayuga Lake, and Sam's mothering, always-comforting cuisine. The only thing missing was a cookbook, and here it is. Enjoy!

Peggy Haine
Greater Trumansburg, 2008

Introduction

Who would have "thunk" it? A simple word like "bistro" filled with controversy!

No one really knows the origin of the word. "Bistro" sounds like a Russian word for speed. It could have come from Russian troops demanding fast service in Paris during Napoleonic times, or the word could stem from a variety of French communities and sources. All that's known about it is that "bistro" first appeared in writing in 1884.

I like "bistro" very much, because it describes a small restaurant that serves moderately priced comforting meals in an unpretentious setting. In other words, a bistro is "down-home," which is how I want Simply Red Bistro to feel. How did I get that way? Easy: I got it from down home. Let me explain.

The low-lying, deeply forested North American Appalachian Mountain range stretches almost unbroken 1,500 miles, taking in Alabama to New England, and all Mid-Atlantic points between. But when most think of its music, we think of the southern section of the region that begins at the Potomac River. Not I. When I think of Appalachian music, I think of South Africa, where I was born.

Back when the word "bistro" was being thought up, the British had taken South Africa from the Dutch. When they did that, the Brits not only planted my Dutch/United Kingdom roots, they planted the sounds of Scottish and Celtic music, counterpart to the Appalachian sounds. I remember, as a little girl, long car trips with my theatrical mom and her musician friends who strummed all the way, and then strummed some more after we reached our destination and it was time for the group to dance.

I also remember standing on a step stool in the kitchen next to my grandmother; to the rhythm of the music I copied her moves, stirring, kneading, and tasting every so often. At four years old, I was making my own lunch!

The food we cooked and ate was varied. My mom was a vegetarian, my maternal grandmother was meat and potatoes Dutch, and my paternal grandmother offered up hearty meals from her Welsh/Celtic roots. But being near the Cape also gave us a Mediterranean influence of seafood and seasonal fare. This cornucopia of good eats infiltrated my DNA, and landed in that compartment right next to where rhythm is stored--in 77 beats per minute, of course. Food and music--down home--became my guide.

When I was 16, my mom took us to Buffalo, New York. There, I broke the borders of family learning when I took a job as a salad bar matron at a Ponderosa Restaurant. I didn't know it then, but I was on my way to quite a culinary adventure. In fact, later at Buffalo University, I studied nutrition with the idea that I would one day become a nutrition and exercise trainer to teach as therapy for food disorders. But university life didn't pan out, and when I arrived as a young woman in Atlanta, Georgia the sound of familiar string instruments made me think of South Africa and the kitchen.

While working the front of the house at the Atlanta branch of the famous Cheesecake Factory Restaurant, a chance at restaurant management training came my way and I jumped at it. For the next five years, I was schooled in the kitchen like I'd never been schooled before. After that experience my DNA said emphatically, "It's a life in food for you, young lady."

It's been a great ride. The Cheesecake Factory took me to Chicago, Pasadena, Westbury, and Boston, where I decided to change gears. In Boston, I went solo and did my first gig as chef at a place called Six Burner Café. But I had been away from my mom and Buffalo for too long. Once again, I went home.

My mom sells Old World musical instruments at the upstate, New York Renaissance Festival, and it's a good thing she does, because that's where I met Gary Izzo. We became an item, and then a team, and for some reason, we wound up in Trumansburg, New York, not far from Ithaca, and later became husband and wife. For some other reason--providence?--we stumbled upon a restaurant space for sale in Trumansburg. That was the start of Simply Red Bistro.

Those readers local to Ithaca and Trumansburg might remember the strumming that emanated on Wednesday nights from a place called The Rongovian Embassy. When I first heard the music, I recalled the Silver Creek Mountain Band of South Africa, and I just knew I had to have some of that music at my restaurant. In fact, I wanted a community night at my restaurant, with music and dancing. Richie Stearns, leader of The Evil City String Band that played at the Rongovian suggested the usually dark Monday night for our communal happening. I took it and them, and have never looked back.

After four years, success was within reach in Trumansburg. I could feel it. But then, we suddenly lost our lease after the building owner decided to sell it.

What to do?

This is where Sheldrake Point Winery comes into my story. In November 2006, we made a deal. Simply Red Bistro would become a part of the winery. Monday community night was rekindled and success once again promised to become reality. But after the Trumansburg experience, I had to ask myself: what exactly is success?

I'm a simple gal. Success for me is cooking what I want to cook, listening to the music I want to hear, and providing a place and atmosphere for a community to flourish. By that measure, I feel successful.

Success also means sharing experiences with others, which is why I've paired the following stories with recipes from my Monday night menus at the restaurant.

I hope you enjoy your Monday nights as much as I enjoy mine.

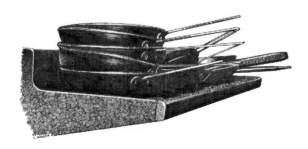

Beverages

"Simply" Red Tea

Truth be told, while most Southerners have probably never heard of rooibos tea, it's a great way to elevate their beloved iced tea. Afrikaans for "red bush," rooibos is harvested in the mountains of South Africa, its leaves oxidized in a process that produces the distinctive reddish-brown color and enhances subtle nutty, toffee, and chocolate flavors. Since it's slightly sweet, even without sugar, iced tea drinkers will enjoy strong, unsweetened rooibos. On the other hand, it's also delicious Southern-style (with enough sugar to curl your toes). Like a good wine, rooibos improves with age. Leftover tea can be stored in the fridge without clouding and re-used at a later time.

For unsweetened tea:

Put tea bags in a heatproof pitcher. In a saucepan bring water and baking soda almost to a boil and pour over tea bags. Steep tea 30 minutes and remove tea bags (do not squeeze). Cool tea and chill, covered, until cold, about 1 hour. Fill 6 pint glass with ice. Pour tea over ice and serve with lemon.

Makes 6 servings.

For sweetened tea:

Fill 2 pint glass with ice. Add the simple syrup and unsweetened tea and stir.

Squeeze the lemon over the ice and tea and enjoy.

Makes 2 servings.

For unsweetened tea:

6 rooibos tea bags

6 cups water

pinch of baking soda

6 lemon wedges

For sweet tea:

16 ounces unsweetened tea

3 teaspoons simple syrup (simmer 1/4 cup water and 1/4 cup granulated white sugar on low heat until the sugar dissolves)

2 lemon wedges

ice cubes

MAMA SAYS...

Sweet tea is the "house wine" of the South, where it's not just a summertime drink, but served year-round with most meals. Southern restaurants will place a pitcher of sweet tea on the table for an entire dinner party to share, and keep refilling it for free.

Iced Coffee

The Southern secret for iced coffee is cane syrup in place of granulated sugar. Caramelized, concentrated syrup that remains after cane juice is boiled to extract sugar, cane syrup is an acquired taste--deeply sweet and slightly bitter. Produced in Abbeville, Louisianna by C. S. Steen's Syrup Mill since 1910, cane syrup can be ordered online at www. steensyrup.com.

Fill 2 pint glasses with crushed ice. Whisk together the cane syrup, coffee and half and half. Pour over the ice and serve.

4 cups brewed coffee
4 ounces half and half
3 ounces Steen's cane syrup
crushed ice

Makes 2 servings.

MAMA SAYS...

Soppin' means dipping biscuits in cane syrup that has butter mashed up in it. You add room temperature butter to a shallow dish, pour the syrup over the butter, and mash them together with a fork. Then dip your biscuit in the mixture, take a bite, and wash it down with iced coffee.

Soda Fountain Lemonade

Lemonade is the sweet Southern refreshment, a staple of old-time pharmacy soda fountains. To make really good lemonade, you need to get all the juice and pulp out of the lemons. Roll whole lemons on the counter to break up pulp and get the most juice. Cut lemons in half and squeeze on a citrus juicer until all the juice is removed. Strain to remove seeds. Crushed mint adds a fragrant, minty flavor, and mint sprigs make a sophisticated garnish.

Whisk together the lemon juice, sugar and hot water. Pour into a glass pitcher filled with the crushed ice and mint and serve.

Makes 1 gallon.

2 cups lemon juice, from fresh-squeezed lemons

1-1/2 cups white granulated sugar

1 gallon hot water

20 mint leaves, medium sized, rough-chopped

10 mint sprigs, whole

crushed ice

MAMA SAYS...

If you pour half a glass of lemonade and half a glass of unsweetened iced tea, you'll have what Southerners call "Half and Half," and what Northerners call an "Arnold Palmer."

Porch Swing Cocktail

Southern Comfort, the fruit, spice, and whiskey-flavored liqueur, was developed by bartender Martin Wilkes Heron at McCauley's Tavern in the French Quarter of New Orleans, Louisiana. With Southern Comfort as her main ingredient, this cocktail formula was developed by bartender Leah Houghtaling at Felicia's Atomic Lounge in Ithaca, New York.

Fill 2 pint glasses with the ice. Pour in the Southern Comfort and ice tea. Squeezed a lemon wedge over the top of each and serve.

Makes 2 servings.

16 ounces sweet tea (recipe pg. 9)
1 ounce Southern Comfort
2 lemon wedges
ice cubes

Well, I declare, with one sip your guests will be transported to a porch swing on the verandah.

MAMA SAYS...

Mint Julep

New Orleans native Truman Capote wrote that "there is nothing better than a mint julep to bring relief from the pressures and pains of summertime." No other cocktail is more often associated with the South, and it's difficult to disprove the claim of Southerners that the mint julep is the world's most civilized and refreshing drink. Juleps are traditionally served in silver or pewter mugs to obtain better frosting.

Divide the bourbon, mint and sugar between two 10-ounce rocks glasses (or pewter mugs) and muddle. Fill the glasses almost to the top with shaved ice, packing down firmly. Garnish each with a mint sprig.

Makes 2 servings.

2 teaspoons white granulated sugar

30 mint leaves

4 ounces Makers Mark (or other good bourbon)

crushed ice

MAMA SAYS...

For crushed ice, put whole ice cubes in a clean tea towel and smash the hell out of it on the kitchen counter.

Sangaree

It's a Southern cousin to traditional sangria, the wine-based fruit punch that originated in Spain. Marinating oranges, peaches and apples in brandy and Cointreau add a wallop to this recipe, so take care, it can go down fast!

Place all ingredients except the champagne in a glass jar and allow it to sit for at least 4 hours in the fridge. Fill 8 wine glasses half-full with ice. Top each glass with a ladle of the base, including some of the fruit. Top off with 1 ounce of sparkling wine and serve.

Makes 8 servings.

2 cups white wine

2 ounces Cointreau (or orange-flavored liqueur)

1 ounces brandy

1/2 apples sliced thin, skin on

1/2 oranges sliced thin, skin on

2 ounces orange juice

1/2 15-ounce can cling peaches, strain off the juice and reserve

2 ounces peach juice from the can of peaches

8 ounces sparkling wine

MAMA SAYS...

Have fun creating your own version of sangria. Start off with my recipe and make changes to suit your own taste. Don't waste expensive wines for this drink. Any white table wine will do. And for goodness sake, top with a cheap sparkling wine, not Champagne.

Hot Cocoa with Ginger-Chipotle Cream

Southern tables are more often enjoying the Mexican and South American influences of comforting cocoas, warmed with "ancient spices." This recipe evokes a time when the Aztecs would brew a strong chocolate beverage spiked with fiery local chili peppers.

In a stand mixer, whip the heavy cream until the cream begins to form stiff peaks. Add the ground ginger, smoked chipotle peppers, and sugar, and continue mixing to thoroughly combine. In a 10-ounce mug, mix the cocoa powder with the remaining chili powder, smoked chipotle peppers and hot water. Make a slurry first with the cocoa powder and a little of the hot water, then add in the rest of the hot water, stirring until smooth. Top the hot cocoa with the whipped cream and garnish with toasted pumpkin seeds. Serve in a tempered 12-ounce mug.

Makes 1 serving.

- 1/4 cup heavy whipping cream
- 1/8 teaspoon ground ginger
- 1/8 teaspoon smoked chipotle peppers in adobe sauce
- 1 teaspoon granulated sugar
- 3-1/2 ounces cocoa powder
- 1/8 teaspoon chili powder
- 1/8 teaspoon smoked chipotle peppers in adobe sauce
- 10 ounces hot water
- 2 ounces pumpkin seeds, toasted

I suggest using Ghirardelli Double Chocolate Hot Cocoa in this recipe since it's easy to find, but you can use any high-quality cocoa, the darker the better.

From the Pantry

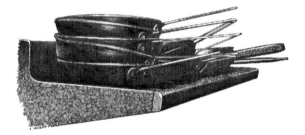

Essential Spice Blends

The underpinnings of southern cuisine are spices and spice blends. No pantry is complete without the right seasonings for richer, more authentic flavors. Over the years I've expanded the borders of my own culinary geography by creating signature spice blends and utilizing them for a range of recipes. Pre-mixing ensures that my line cooks are preparing dishes with consistency, and likewise will provide more confident cooking in your home kitchen.

MAMA SAYS...

When blending spices, measure ingredients accurately and mix thoroughly in a metal bowl. To preserve peak flavor and freshness, store in a cool, dry place, away from exposure to bright light or moisture, and not too close to the stove or oven. Allow spice mixtures to mellow for 24 hours before using them, so that the ingredients can balance out.

Herb Mix

Like spouses in a good marriage, spices complement each other when they are properly combined. This is my "mother" composition, each spoonful adding extra life to favorite dishes and other blends.

Makes 2-1/2 cups.

Ingredients for Herb Mix:

1/2 cup oregano

1/2 cup basil

1/2 cup thyme

1/2 cup sea salt

1/2 cup ground black pepper

Barbeque Spice

The art of barbeque requires combining a range of different kinds of tastes and textures together to create an ideal balance that tantalizes the taste buds. Developed over many years of trials, my savory blend adds heat and aromatics to anything you want to barbeque or grill. Also use in Moroccan or West African recipes.

Ingredients for Barbeque Spice:
1-1/4 cups herb mix (recipe p. 20)
1/4 cup brown mustard seed
1/4 cup ground cumin
1/4 cup ground coriander
1/4 cup ground cinnamon
1/4 cup ground nutmeg
1/2 cup ground ginger
1/2 cup ground cloves

Makes 3-1/2 cups plus 2 tablespoons.

Cajun Spice

My variation is great for the "blackening" lover in all of us: sprinkle on both sides of steak, chicken, and seafood, and pan fry. Use it as the base for a Southern-style shrimp cocktail sauce.

Makes 1 cup.

Ingredients for Cajun Spice:

10 tablespoons barbeque spice (recipe p. 21)

2 tablespoons cayenne

4 tablespoons paprika

Curry Spice

Adding turmeric and cumin to the traditional Indian spice blend, garam masala, further enhances the flavor of a dish's main ingredients. A small spoonful is enough to provide richness and fullness to curries, sauces, and chicken salad.

Ingredients for Curry Spice:

1 cup turmeric

1 cup cumin

1 cup garam masala

Makes 1-1/2 cups.

Breads

Kickass Cornbread

This is Southern cornbread the way God intended it--with a bit of sugar for sweetening, grated cheddar cheese, and smoked chipotle peppers for a smoky, spicy kick--comfort food for the soul. Bake up a batch and enjoy the toasty aroma as it fills the kitchen. Then whip up some honey butter and slather it on with abandon.

Combine the cornmeal, flour, sugar, salt and baking powder in one bowl. In a separate bowl whisk together milk, oil, eggs, cheddar and chipotle peppers. Pour the wet mixture into the dry mixture and mix with a wooden spoon until just combined. Scrape into pan with a spatula (use non-stick spray) and place in the oven on the center rack. Bake in pre-heated oven at 375-degrees for 30 minutes until a toothpick comes out clean. Cool, slice into chunks and serve with honey butter.

Makes 8 servings.

2 cups cornmeal

2 cups flour

1/4 cup white granulated sugar

1 tablespoon salt

2 tablespoons baking powder

2 cups whole milk

1/2 cup canola oil

2 eggs

1 cup grated cheddar

3 tablespoons smoked chipotle peppers, chopped, in adobe sauce

MAMA SAYS...

Use muffin or cornstick pans (preferably iron), to vary the shape. Instead of baking, try frying the batter like pancakes.

Rustic Flatbread

There is something immediately comforting about home-baked bread. Taking in deep breaths of freshly baking bread is aromatherapy for the senses, and a chef can experience the same cravings, the same satisfaction as anyone else. I love this country-style descendent of Italian focaccia for its endless garnishing possibilities, usually inspired by leftover ingredients from the previous night's dinner. One of my favorite versions includes caramelized onions with sage and blue cheese crumbles.

Step 1: whisk these ingredients together until foamy. Let stand 10 minutes. Pour into a stand mixer with bread hook.

Step 2: add the flour slowly to the mixer, then add 3 tablespoons of olive oil and the salt. Mix until the dough comes together, and continue to knead the dough for 5 minutes. Drizzle the remaining 1 tablespoon of olive oil on the cookie sheet. Place the dough on metal cookie sheet tray and allow to rise for 20 minutes. Flip over, squish down, and allow to rise another 15 minutes.

Step 3: in a heated pan, add the olive oil and onions, and cook until the onions are a light golden brown, then deglaze the pan with the balsamic vinegar. Add the sage and sauté for an additional 2 minutes. Let it cool slightly then spread over the dough. Crumble the blue cheese over the top. Place in a pre-heated oven and bake for 15 minutes at 375-degrees. Allow to cool slightly, sprinkle with the sea salt, slice and serve.

Makes 6 servings.

Ingredients for Step 1:

1 cup water, at 105-degrees (if you don't have a thermometer, it's the same as bath water)

1 heaping tablespoon quick active yeast for bread

1 tablespoon honey

Ingredients for Step 2:

3 cups flour

4 tablespoons olive oil

1 teaspoon salt

Ingredients for Step 3:

1 onion sliced thin

2 tablespoons olive oil

2 tablespoons balsamic vinegar

1 tablespoon fresh sage

1 teaspoon sea salt

MAMA SAYS...

Topping flatbread is an art in itself, so be creative! You can add a bit of fresh basil and thyme, or you can pile on the toppings to create what amounts to a thick-crusted pizza.

Drop Biscuits with Cheddar & Black Pepper

Buttermilk does the trick in these savory, cheddar-flecked biscuits with the surprise of fresh-ground black pepper to pep you up and make you smile. Make it a meal. These biscuits are best served smothered with a slow-cooked beef stew or chicken and biscuits.

Mix flour, baking powder, sugar, salt and black pepper. Whisk together the buttermilk, butter, egg and cheddar. Pour into the dry mix and mix just until incorporated. Spray a baking sheet with non sick spray, scoop and loose-drop the biscuit batter onto the tray. In a pre-heated oven, bake for 7 to 10 minutes at 400-degrees, until they feel dry. Serve with unsalted butter.

Makes 10 small or 6 large biscuits.

2 cups flour

1 tablespoon baking powder

2 teaspoons white sugar

1 teaspoon salt

1 teaspoon fresh ground black pepper

1 cup buttermilk

3 tablespoons melted butter

1 egg

1 cup cheddar cheese, grated

MAMA SAYS...

Aged English cheddars work fabulously in this recipe, drier and easy to grate. If you want a less-assertive cheese, try reducing the cheddar amount or substitute another grating cheese like Parmigiano Reggiano.

Down-Home Buttermilk Biscuits

Nothing tastes better than homemade strawberry jam on warm biscuits--hot out of the oven. In our house, my mom would serve buttermilk biscuits as a part of our ritual every Sunday morning, layered with strawberry jam and cream. The real secret to getting a good rise out of your biscuits is to get a clean cut with a biscuit cutter. And don't twist the cutter as you cut out the biscuits. They rise higher without the twist. Morning, noon, or night, a buttermilk biscuit hits the spot.

Place flour in a large mixing bowl, then add the grated butter, baking powder, and salt. Using the tips of your fingers blend in the butter until the mixture is in large crumbles. Add in the eggs and buttermilk until just blended. Press the mixture together until it forms a ball. Gently press the dough out onto the surface using a biscuit cutter and press out 6 biscuits. Place onto a non-stick baking tray 2 inches apart. Bake in a 425-degree oven for 10-12 minutes, until light brown. Serve with fresh whipped cream and jam.

1 pound of flour

1 stick of unsalted butter, grated

2 tablespoons baking powder

1/4 teaspoon salt

2 eggs

1/2 cup buttermilk

12 ounces strawberry jam

1 cup heavy cream for whipping

Makes 6 servings.

MAMA SAYS...

The preferred pan for the baking of biscuits is a biscuit pan – a sheet pan which has about 1/2- inch raised edges. It should be a bright, shiny pan. A dark pan will cause the biscuits to brown too much on their bottoms. (A substitution for buttermilk: ½ cup milk with 2 teaspoons of white vinegar).

"Dead Banana" Bread

Plan ahead a few days before making banana bread, because the most important ingredient is over-ripe (black-ripe), very soft, mushy bananas, or according to my 3-year-old daughter Madi, they must be "dead." Moist banana bread is a favorite for tea time, snack or coffee break.

In a stand mixer with the paddle attachment, cream the butter and sugar. Add in the eggs one at a time then the vanilla, flour, baking soda, salt and buttermilk. Continue to mix until just combined, then add in the bananas and the walnuts. Pour the batter into a loaf tin coated with non stick spray and bake in a pre-heated oven for 45 minutes to 1 hour at 350-degrees, until a knife inserted comes out clean.

Makes 6 servings.

1 stick butter

3/4 cup granulated white sugar

2 eggs

1 teaspoon vanilla

1 cup flour

1 teaspoon baking soda

1 teaspoon salt

3 tablespoons buttermilk

3 large over ripe bananas

1/2 cup walnuts, toasted for 5 minutes in a 350-degree oven

MAMA SAYS...

I like to toast the nuts for banana bread, since it adds a nice and toasty flavor. Serve with a generous spread of honey butter.

Double-Corn & Zucchini Spoon Bread

Spoon bread, a cross between corn bread and soufflé, is a vital part of Southern cultural and culinary tradition. It starts out on the stovetop, spends some time in the oven, then graces the dinner table for everyone to enjoy. Spoon bread has a light, soft, pudding-like consistency and (you guessed it) should be eaten with a spoon. The core ingredient is cornmeal, but the addition of corn off the cob and grated zucchini adds a lot to the dish.

Bring milk, cornmeal, corn kernels, zucchini, butter and salt to boil in a heavy 3 quart saucepan over medium heat, stirring frequently, and simmer until thickened, 3 to 4 minutes. Remove from heat and cool, then whisk in the egg yolks. Beat egg whites and a pinch of salt with an electric mixer at medium speed just until soft peaks form. Fold in gently to the corn mixture. Spread into a buttered 9 ½ inch-deep dish and bake in the center of a pre-heated oven at 425-degrees until puffed and golden, 15 to 20 minutes. Serve immediately.

2 cups whole milk

1/3 cup cornmeal

1-1/2 cups fresh corn kernels from 2-3 ears of corn

1-1/2 cups fresh zucchini grated

1 tablespoon butter

2 teaspoons salt

4 large eggs, separated

Makes 6 servings.

MAMA SAYS...

Is spoon bread a bread or a side dish? Let's just say it's a winning combination of both, delicious alongside fried chicken, barbeque chicken, or roasted chicken.

Hushpuppies

African immigrants living in the American South find reminders of their ancestral homeland throughout the region's cuisine. For instance, hushpuppies derive from a West African streetfood called "akara." The best hushpuppies are crusty outside and tender inside--they need to be cooked, but not too hard. Here's my enhanced version of the good old Southern-style quick bread.

In a mixing bowl, combine all the dry ingredients, then create a well in the center of the mix and add the wet ingredients. Mix both together until just combined. (The batter can be made two hours in advance, covered and kept in a fridge until needed). Heat oil in a heavy bottom half-gallon pot, or a pot that is at least twice the volume of the oil. Use a candy thermometer to monitor the temperature of the oil at 350-degrees. Once the oil has reached temperature, drop tablespoon-sized drops of dough into the oil. (I work in batches of 6 at a time). Use another tablespoon to help push the dough off the spoon into the oil so as not to make a big splash of oil (work carefully as the oil is very hot). Fry for 10 minutes until they float to the top, turning as they fry, then use a pair of tongs to pull them out of the oil. Set on a paper towel to absorb the excess oil. (They can be kept in a 250 degree oven warm until all the batches have been fried). Serve on a platter with whipped honey butter.

- 1-3/4 cups cornmeal
- 1/2 cup flour
- 1 tablespoon granulated white sugar
- 2 teaspoons baking powder
- 1 teaspoon salt
- 1/2 teaspoon baking soda
- 1 egg
- 1 cup buttermilk
- 1/2 cup sliced green onions
- 1/4 cup warm water
- 8 cups vegetable oil or peanut oil for frying
- honey butter

Makes 24 pieces.

MAMA SAYS...

The name "hushpuppies" is often attributed to hunters or fisherman who would quickly fry cornmeal and feed it to their dogs to "hush the puppies" during cookouts or fish frys.

Cracked Wheat Rolls

Bulgur is made from wheat kernels that are steamed and toasted before cracking, so that they develop a rich, nutty flavor. Cracked wheat adds a chewy, rustic character to these rolls.

Place the bulgur wheat in a saucepan with 2 cups of water, bring to a boil and simmer until bulgur is tender and then let it cool. Whisk together the warm milk, yeast and honey and let it rest until foamy. Turn mixer to low speed and add the yeast mixture, eggs, oats, whole wheat flour, black pepper, salt and olive oil. Add the white flour in 1/2 cup increments until well incorporated and the dough springs back. Place in a large bowl, cover with plastic and let rise 1-2 hours in a warm place until doubled in volume. In a 10-inch spring form pan, divide the dough into 12 equal-sized balls, cover and let it rise again until doubled in size. Once risen, sprinkle the top of the dough with olive oil and sprinkle mixed seeds over the top. Pre-heat oven to 375-degrees. Bake until golden brown (about 20-22 minutes) until an inserted toothpick comes out clean. Serve with butter.

- 1/2 cup bulgur wheat
- 1 cup warm milk (105 degrees)
- 2 tablespoons dry yeast
- 1/3 cup honey
- 2 eggs
- 1/4 cup quick cooking oats
- 1-1/4 cups whole wheat flour
- 1 teaspoon black pepper
- 1 tablespoon salt
- 2-1/2 - 3-1/2 cups white flour
- 2 tablespoon olive oil
- 3 tablespoons mixed seeds: fennel, caraway, poppy, salt and pepper

Makes 12 rolls.

MAMA SAYS...

I created these rolls a number of years ago, even before I became a chef, and a few of my mom's friends have been begging for the recipe ever since. I've always explained that they would have to wait for my cookbook. So, my dears, here's the long-awaited secret formula! Enjoy with soup or my veggie chili.

VetKoek

Pronounced "fetcook," the Afrikaans name means "fat cake," a fried dough, shaped like a small ball. The history of this traditional pastry goes back many years, to the days of the early Voortrekkers who found it quicker and easier to make than bread.

In a metal mixing bowl, sift together the dry ingredients, then add in the wet ingredients and combine into a stiff dough. Heat oil in a heavy-bottom 1 gallon pot, or a pot that is at least twice the volume of the oil. Use a candy thermometer to monitor the temperature of the oil at 350-degrees. Once the oil has reached temperature, drop tablespoon sized drops of dough into the oil. (I work in batches of 6 at a time). Use another tablespoon to help push the dough off the spoon into the oil so as not to make a big splash of oil, work carefully as the oil is very hot. Fry for 10 minutes, or until they float to the top, then use a pair of tongs to pull them out of the oil. They can be kept in a 250-degree oven warm until all batches have been fried. Serve with butter and jam.

- 1-3/4 cups flour
- 2 teaspoons baking powder
- 1 tablespoon white granulated sugar
- 1/2 teaspoon salt
- 2 beaten eggs
- 1/2 cup whole milk
- 4 cups vegetable or peanut oil, for frying

Makes 12 cakes.

MAMA SAYS...

During my childhood in South Africa, these cakes were a regular part of meals on my great-grandmother's farm. As soon as they're out of the fryer, I can hardly wait to break them open and slather with strawberry jam and gobs of butter.

Malay Roti

Dishes inherited from South Africa's early Malaysian immigrants include this crispy on the outside, fluffy on the inside flatbread, an essential companion to contemporary curries.

Combine both flours and salt in a bowl. Add butter and rub with your fingers to form a crumbly mixture. Add water and mix to a soft dough. Knead, adding flour to make an even-textured, pliable dough. Allow to rest for 30 minutes, covered in a bowl with a towel. Divide dough into 8 pieces. Roll into a small ball and leave covered again. Roll out into quarter-inch thick circles. Heat a heavy-based frying pan and fry the rotis one at a time with a little oil in the pan, turning occasionally and brushing with the butter and oil mixture. Fry until golden brown and speckled.

3 cups cake flour

1/3 cup self-raising flour

1 teaspoon salt

3 tablespoon butter

1 cup cold water

1/3 cup flour

4 tablespoon melted butter
    mixed with 4 tablespoons
    oil

Makes 8 servings.

MAMA SAYS...

The original roti is a plain (tasty nevertheless), however in Malaysia, it's transformed to include fillings from bananas, butter, eggs, to other more exotic flavors.

Sauces/Butters

Cajun Remoulade

In the best tradition of New Orleans "tartar sauce," my remoulade (pronounced "ruma-lahd") has a full-flavored zip that will really get your taste buds jumping. My own spin on the classic is mayonnaise-based, then spiked with capers and spice mix. I love to serve it with catfish and fried green tomatoes, but don't stop there. It partners well with a variety of vegetables, cold meats, and fish, especially shellfish.

Whisk all ingredients together in a small metal bowl. Store in the fridge (in an air tight container) for at least several hours before serving.

Makes 1 cup.

1 cup mayonnaise

1/2 tablespoon Cajun spice (recipe p. 22)

1/2 tablespoon capers, with some juice

MAMA SAYS...

Before serving, bring the sauce to cool room temperature to bring out more flavor.

Curry Mayonnaise

Both Creole and Cajun cooks are adept at using whatever's on hand and experimenting with seasonings and other ingredients. The idea is to taste the spices involved without burning the palate, and mayonnaise comes to life when accented by the smoky heat of curry powder. It's great as a dip for sweet potato fries or as a substitute for plain old mayonnaise in chicken and tuna salads.

Whisk all ingredients together in a metal mixing bowl. Store in an airtight container.

Makes 1-1/2 cups.

1-1/2 cups mayonnaise
1 tablespoon curry spice blend
(recipe p. 23)

MAMA SAYS...

This is better if served several hours after making it or the next day when all of the flavors have blended together well.

Roasted Garlic-Lemon Aioli

Bless those French colonizers who arrived in New Orleans with "butter of Provence," the flavorful garlic mayonnaise that adds so much to Southern cuisine. You can make your own mayo, then make this sauce, or just go ahead and use store-bought mayonnaise as its base. It's great with a veggie burger, garlic-and-herb fries, or wherever you'd use mayo. The strength of the garlic and acidity of the lemon make this a wonderfully balanced addition to any dish.

Slice the garlic and cover with the oil in a microwaveable container, heat for 20 seconds at a time until the garlic is soft and can be mashed with a fork. Drain oil. Mix all ingredients in food processor with blade attachment until well combined, smooth and creamy. Store in fridge until needed.

1 cup mayonnaise, at room temperature

2 teaspoons herb mix

1 tablespoon lemon juice

2 cloves garlic

2 tablespoons olive oil

MAMA SAYS...

Quality of the garlic is very important. It should be fresh and plump with swollen cloves. Discard any shriveled cloves or any in which the core is developing a green sprout.

Orange-Chipotle Vinaigrette

Basic vinaigrette can be expanded on in infinite ways. In a version I created for a Mexican-theme dinner, orange adds a fresh, bright taste while smoky chipotle adds the jazz. We served it over mixed greens with grated cheddar cheese, black beans, avocado, toasted pumpkin seeds, sliced banana chips, red onions and sprouts.

Place all the ingredients in a food processor with blade attachment, except for the oil. Turn on and allow it to mix for a few seconds, then gradually add the oil until it has all come together (emulsified). Pour into a glass jar and keep in the refrigerator until needed.

Makes 4 cups.

2 tablespoons honey

2 tablespoons whole grain mustard

2 tablespoons herb mix (recipe p. 20)

3-1/2 ounces smoked chipotle in adobo

2 tablespoons orange juice

1/2 cup cider vinegar

1 ounce garlic cloves, peeled

3 cups blended oil (half canola and half olive oil)

MAMA SAYS...

More than just a dressing for vegetable salads, it doubles as a marinade for shrimp, chicken or grilled steak.

Best Damn Barbeque Sauce

It starts out with a savory flavor from the tomatoes and toasty notes from the coffee, followed by robust, bittersweet black strap molasses and punctuated with chili peppers in the finish. It's the complex layering of flavors in this sauce that's so lip teasin' and palate pleasin'--a distinctively Southern blend of thickness, hotness, sweetness, and tartness.

Whisk all ingredients together in a bowl. Store in an air-tight container in the fridge.

Makes 5 cups.

1-1/4 cups white onion, chopped

2 cloves of garlic, crushed and chopped into small pieces

3 cups ketchup

1 cup honey

1/4 cup Worcestershire

1/4 cup soy sauce

2 tablespoons smoked chipotle chilis, in adobo

1 cup coffee

1/2 cup blackstrap molasses

MAMA SAYS...

I use this adventurous sauce on our veggie burgers and as the base for our chili. I know you will find lots of great uses for it. It will keep well in the fridge in an airtight container.

Honey Butter

Honey contributes warm, natural sweetness while butter distributes the sweetness over your bread or food of choice with even precision. Local honey and artisanal butter whipped together create a heavenly spread, yummy when slathered over muffins, biscuits, cornbread or scones. Let the butter sit out overnight to let it soften, then blend with honey in a mixer. It will keep a little longer than a regular stick of butter in the fridge.

Place butter into stand mixer with the paddle attachment. Whip the butter on medium speed until it has changed from an off-yellow color to white. Turn off the mixer. Add honey and whip a few more minutes. Scrape out and store in fridge.

1 pound unsalted butter, room temperature, cut into cubes

1 cup local honey

MAMA SAYS...

A baked sweet potato with honey butter will make dinner taste a little bit better tonight.

Garlic Herb Butter

If you're tired of serving the same old slab of butter at dinner, you can jazz up your meal by simply adding a few fresh ingredients. The strength of raw garlic and the balance of fresh herbs compliment each other in a topping that's great on hand-cut fries, pasta, or steamed vegetables. Actually, it's hard to find anything this butter is not good on.

Place all ingredients in food processor with blade attachment and pulse until all ingredients are incorporated and evenly blended. Place herb butter mix into a small saucepan and heat on low until melted.

1 pound butter at room temperature, cut into cubes
1/4 cup chopped garlic cloves
1 cup chopped parsley
1 cup chopped cilantro
1 cup chopped basil
1 tablespoon herb mix (recipe p. 20)

MAMA SAYS...

"Garlic is as good as ten mothers," according to Les Blank's affectionate film homage to the bountiful bulb.

Dried Fruit Chutney

Dried fruits, eaten whole or simmered in vinegar and brown sugar to a jam-like consistency, are nutritious comfort foods in my native South Africa.

Place all ingredients in a pot and simmer on low for 1 hour. Cool and store until ready to serve.

Makes 6 cups.

1 cup dried apricot, sliced into strips

1 cup dried figs, cut in half

1 cup raisins

1 cup dates, cut in to smaller pieces

4 cups cider vinegar

1 tablespoon red chili flakes

4 cloves of garlic, diced

3 cups brown sugar

1 tablespoon salt

This recipe can be made days in advance and kept in the refrigerator. It will keep for a month. I use this spicy chutney to accompany a number of grain dishes or serve as a sandwich spread.

Salads and
Dressings

Kicked-Up Coleslaw

American coleslaw evolved from a hot cabbage salad made by early Dutch settlers. Here's my sassy take on the often humdrum side-dish, sweetened with plump raisins and brightened by cilantro. It's a perfect partner with ribs, smoked chicken, and a must with my Cornmeal-Crusted Catfish. Use it as an ingredient on barbecue sandwiches, even on hamburgers or hot dogs along with chili and hot mustard.

In a metal bowl, whisk together the mayonnaise, honey, vinegar and salt. Set mandolin (or other slicer) on the lowest setting (for very thin slices), and shred the cabbages. Toss cabbage in a chilled bowl with the carrots, raisins and cilantro. Add dressing, mix all ingredients together, and serve.

Makes 6 servings.

8 cups of shredded white cabbage

2 cups shredded purple cabbage

1 cup grated carrots

1 cup mayonnaise

2 tablespoons honey

2 teaspoons cider vinegar

2 teaspoons sea salt

1/3 cup plump raisins

1/4 cup chopped cilantro

MAMA SAYS...

Dress just before serving to maintain maximum crispness.

BLT Iceberg Wedge

Filmmaker John Waters calls iceberg lettuce "the polyester of greens." He may hate it, but I love it--especially when a fresh wedge is dressed with tomatoes, bacon, and creamy blue cheese dressing. It's a great starter salad to an evening of barbeque, good company, and cocktails.

For the bacon:

Sprinkle bacon with Cajun spice and bake in the oven for 15 to 20 minutes at 350-degrees. Drain the fat, cool and chop.

For the salad:

Place 1 wedge of iceberg lettuce onto each of 4 plates. Drizzle blue cheese dressing over the greens (approx. 4-ounces per salad). Sprinkle bacon pieces, tomatoes, croutons and extra blue cheese crumbles over the top. Add a pinch of Cajun spice to the top of each salad. Serve immediately with fresh-ground pepper.

Makes 4 servings.

For the bacon:

8 strips bacon

2 tablespoons Cajun spice (recipe p. 22)

For the salad:

1 head of iceberg lettuce, cut into 4 wedges

16 ounces creamy blue cheese dressing (recipe on p. 51)

8 strips of spiced bacon, baked & chopped

1 cup croutons (1/4 cup per salad, store bought are fine)

4 Roma tomatoes, cut into small wedges (1 tomato per salad)

4 ounces blue cheese, crumbled (1 ounce per salad)

pinch of Cajun spice (recipe p. 22)

black pepper, freshly cracked

The return of crunchy iceberg lettuce to restaurant menus is a trend I embrace. It makes the best summer salad of all.

Creamy Blue Cheese Dressing

This rich and creamy blue cheese dressing is a bold topping that balances the cool, crisp crunch of iceberg. Its intense interplay of flavors stands up to the Cajun persuasion of my BLT Iceberg Wedge.

In a food processor, place the garlic, white vinegar, lemon juice, anchovies, herb mix, eggs, mustard and sugar. Turn it on to medium speed and slowly add the olive oil, allowing it to emulsify. Scrape out into a metal bowl and whisk in the crumbled blue cheese. Store in an air tight container in the fridge.

Makes 5 cups.

2 cloves of garlic

1/2 cup white vinegar

2 tablespoons lemon juice

3 anchovies

1 tablespoon herb mix (recipe p. 20)

2 eggs

1/2 tablespoon whole grain mustard

1 tablespoon white sugar

3-1/2 cups blended olive and canola oil

1 cup blue cheese crumbles

MAMA SAYS...

The recipe has raw egg in it, so it should only be kept no longer than a week in the fridge.

Glorified Potato Eater's Salad

There's been an evolution in my recipe for this dish, as I've adjusted the balance of ingredients. One thing I learned a long time ago from my Mom was to mix the base dressing mix with the potatoes while they are still warm. This draws dressing into the potatoes, more than just coating the outsides as most recipes call for.

For the potatoes:
Add potatoes to a large pot with enough salted cold water to cover. Place on the stove at medium-high heat and cook for 20 minutes, until an inserted knife goes through the potato easily. Drain and allow to cool slightly (potatoes should still be warm when you mix them with the dressing).

For the bacon:
Sprinkle bacon with Cajun spice and bake in the oven for 15 minutes at 350-degrees. Drain the fat, cool and chop.

For the salad:
Mix mayonnaise, mustard, barbeque spices, red onion, celery, and bacon in a metal bowl. Peel the eggs, chop and toss into the mayonnaise mix. Toss with the potatoes once they are cool enough to handle. Cover with plastic and chill in the fridge. Sprinkle parsley and Cajun spice just before serving.
Makes 8 servings.

For the potatoes:
2 ½ pounds red potatoes quartered bite size
2 tablespoons sea salt

For the bacon:
4 strips bacon
1 tablespoon Cajun spice (recipe p. 22)

For the salad:
2 ½ pounds potatoes, boiled & sliced
2 eggs, hard-boiled
4 strips of spiced bacon, baked & chopped
1 cup mayonnaise
1 tablespoon whole grain mustard
1/2 teaspoon each barbeque spice and herb mix (recipe on pg)
1/4 cup diced red onion
1 cup thin sliced celery
1/4 cup parsley, chopped
1 teaspoon Cajun spice (recipe p. 22)

MAMA SAYS...

I often find my prep cooks dipping into this salad just as its being mixed and the potatoes are still warm. Try it once you will be converted forever.

Caesar Salad

Although there are many ways to make old-fashioned recipes more contemporary, there are certain recipes that should just stay as they are. This is one of them. Caesar salad has become an American comfort food in the last few years, and my version sticks pretty close to the classic. The tangy dressing has the real stuff in it, including anchovies and eggs. When it's married with crisp, slightly-bitter romaine greens and freshly-shaved Parmesan, it becomes a succulent taste experience.

Place garlic, eggs, anchovies, lemon juice and mustard in the food processor.

Turn it on to medium speed and very slowly add the olive oil until ingredients are incorporated. Scrape the dressing into the metal bowl and fold in the cheese and Worcestershire. Store in an air-tight container in the fridge. Tear washed and dried romaine lettuce into large pieces. Place in large bowl, drizzle with dressing and toss to coat evenly. Serve immediately.

Makes 6 servings.

1 garlic clove

1 egg

2 anchovies

1 tablespoon lemon juice

1 teaspoon wholegrain mustard

1 cup olive oil

1/2 cup parmesan cheese, fresh-shaved

1/2 teaspoon Worcestershire

2 heads romaine lettuce

MAMA SAYS...

Rinse the anchovy fillets under cold running water to remove the salty packing oil. Drain well and make sure they are dry before adding to the dressing mix.

Caesar Salad Supreme

The play of flavors and textures is interesting in this entrée salad, between the crunchy croutons, spicy nuts, meaty oysters, and the crunch of romaine leaves. Sharpness of the dressing makes the salad almost intoxicating.

For the spiced nuts:

Roast nuts in 375-degree oven for 10 minutes. Melt the butter and mix in spices and sugar and pour mixture over the nuts upon removal from the oven. Allow to cool on a baking sheet.

For the croutons:

Mix all ingredients together in a bowl. Place onto a cookie sheet and toast in 375-degree oven for 7 to 10 minutes, until crispy. Allow to cool.

For the Cajun cornmeal-crusted oysters:

Heat oil in a deep pan Mix together the cornmeal and Cajun spice. Work in batches of 6 and toss the oysters in the cornmeal. Dust off and place slowly into the oil (they only take 5 seconds to cook, pull out and place onto a paper towel lined plate to cool as you work through the rest of the oysters).

For the salad:

In a mixing bowl, toss the romaine lettuce and the Caesar dressing. Mound the lettuce on 6 plates and sprinkle with cheese. Top with the croutons, spiced nuts and lemon wedges. Top each salad with 6 cornmeal-crusted oysters.

Makes 6 servings.

For the spiced nuts:
1 cup assorted salted mixed nuts
1-1/2 tbsps melted butter
1 tbsp brown sugar
1/8 tsp each cinnamon, ground cumin and red pepper flakes

For the croutons:
2 cups cubed baguette
1/4 cup olive oil
1/2 tbsp Cajun spice (recipe p. 22)

For the Cajun oysters:
3 dozen oysters, fresh-shucked
2 cups cornmeal
1/4 cup Cajun spice (recipe p. 22)
4 cups vegetable oil for frying

For the salad:
2 heads romaine, chopped into one-inch pieces
8 ounces Caesar dressing (recipe p. 53)
2 cups croutons
1 lemon quartered into wedges
1/2 cup parmesan cheese
1 cup spiced nuts
cornmeal-crusted oysters

MAMA SAYS...

It's best to buy the oysters on the very day you plan to serve this salad. Make sure they are fresh, that they do not smell and, if any are open, they will close up with a simple tap.

Watermelon Summer Salad

During the heat of summertime, when the livin' is easy and water-melon season is in full swing, there's hardly a more refreshing side salad to accompany barbeque steak, chicken or fish. Adding olive oil, mint and feta add a depth that takes this salad from a sweet juicy treat to a more balanced savory side.

Toss all ingredients in a mixing bowl and allow to marinate for 30 minutes in the fridge, allowing all the flavors to come together.

Makes 6 servings.

8 cups seedless watermelon, cut into 1-inch, bite-size pieces

1/4 cup fresh mint, chopped fine

1 cup feta cheese, crumbled

1/4 cup olive oil

1 teaspoon salt

1 teaspoon fresh ground black pepper

MAMA SAYS...

If you have any doubts about the combination of feta and watermelon, you'll be convinced after the first bite. The tangy, salty cheese has an ef-fortless and natural affinity with the sweet, juicy melon.

Angry Vinegar

The word "vinegar" derives from the Old French "vin aigre," meaning "sour wine." Distilled white vinegar flourishes with the addition of jalapenos, a tangy dressing for collard greens or whatever else pleases you.

Whisk all ingredients together in a bowl until they are well combined and the sugar has been dissolved. Store in a sealed container in the fridge and use as needed. (A squirt bottle provides easy access and usage).

3 -3/4 cups white vinegar
1 tablespoon sugar
1 teaspoon salt
2 jalapenos, sliced

Makes 4 cups.

MAMA SAYS...

When slicing jalapeno peppers, be sure you use plastic gloves to prevent a painful burn. If your skin becomes exposed to the oil, apply rubbing alcohol with a cotton ball.

About the Winery

Sheldrake Point Vineyard Winery got its start in the 1990s when I visited the Finger Lakes region from my native Ontario, Canada, where I worked at a local winery. After connecting with Greg Sandor, who was trying to buy the farm that is now Sheldrake Point Vineyard, I signed up in 1997 to get the winery into the ground, literally, with the first 5 acres of grapes planted that spring. With the help of another crucial partner, Chuck Tauck, Sheldrake is up from 5 to 44 vineyard acres and producing 9000 cases of wine annually.

Wine and food was built into the Sheldrake concept and one of the other partners, Scott Signori, operated the café, which opened in 1998 along with the winery's tasting room. But the turn of the twenty-first century found Sheldrake Vineyard hosting an in-house café that somehow didn't seem to be working out exactly as planned, and then I got a brainstorm.

I had been eating at Sam's Trumansburg bistro for some time. The food was interesting and eclectic, but most of all, the wine pairings, though unusual, worked quite well with the food and the spicing. It was clear to me that Sam was very hands on and passionately engaged with food, wine and people. I enjoyed the bistro so much that when I found out that Sam had lost her lease I scooted up there immediately to have dinner and to start a conversation.

It turned out that Sam was looking at options--in Ithaca--but that she had also thought about Sheldrake Point as a possibility. We agreed to keep talking and see what would work out. But I didn't want to prolong the conversation and since we were really looking for a major change for our café, and Sam looked like a terrific fit, I brought Chuck Tauck into the talks quickly. After only a couple of meetings, we shook hands and then spent a little time working out the specifics. This was late in 2006. We really wanted to start 2007 with a plan for Sam and Sheldrake Point Vineyard.

Sam was clearly committed to developing her concept and skills for regional foods paired with interesting wines. She was also hands-on, understood a lot about developing a concept and bringing it to fruition.

There was solid evidence that her concept included excellent design. Plus, Simply Red Bistro had community support and loyal customers that were likely to follow her. So Sam came to us as Executive Chef with responsibility for all food service operations including our intensive wedding and private events program.

Simply Red Bistro works well with our 32,000 visitors a year. We try for professionalism across all of our operations and Sam fits well, there, too. The marriage between Simply Red Bistro and Sheldrake Point Vineyard enables both parties to move up the quality ladder, especially in service and scale. It's regional wines and regional foods within an international perspective. More importantly, customer feedback has been positive. They have been universally thrilled with this development.

If a winemaker attracts attention, then a chef attracts even more, especially a chef like Samantha Izzo. The Monday night menu and music at Simply Red Bistro provides the winery with a direct connection to some of the local community and neighbors and so it brings enormous good will to Sheldrake Point Vineyard. It helps that Monday night is more fun than anyone can expect!

Bob Madill,
Sheldrake Point

Appetizers

Fried Green Tomatoes

The first time I ever tasted fried green tomatoes was on a visit to Jazz Fest in New Orleans where they were served over crab cakes between thick slices of French bread. Yum! Unripe tomatoes have a firm texture with a pleasantly acidic bite that I find irresistible, often with just a whisper of tomato flavor. In my version of this dish, a sprinkle of Cajun spice slips in almost surreptitiously, and most of the flavor comes from the accompanying remoulade.

Ingredients:
6 green tomatoes, sliced
2 cups buttermilk
6 cups cornmeal
2 tablespoons salt
2 tablespoons Cajun remoulade per serving (recipe p. 39)
1 cup canola oil
Cajun spice (recipe p. 22)

Place buttermilk in one bowl. Mix the cornmeal and salt and divide between two bowls. With the left hand, place each tomato slice in the cornmeal and shake to cover. Remove with the same hand and place into the buttermilk, shake gently, then use the right hand to remove from the buttermilk and place into the second bowl of cornmeal. Using the left hand, again cover both sides with cornmeal, shake to remove excess, and remove. Place breaded slices on a cookie sheet until ready to fry. Fill a cast iron skillet with a half-inch of canola oil, and heat to medium-high. Place breaded tomato slices gently into the oil so as not to splash and fry 2 minutes on one side, flip over and cook 2 minutes on the other side. Place breaded slices on a cookie sheet tray. Place in a pre-heated oven set at 350-degrees for 5 minutes to reheat and crisp. Serve 4 tomatoes on each plate with 2 tablespoons of remoulade. Sprinkle with Cajun spice and serve.

Makes 6 servings.

MAMA SAYS...

Set up a "dipping station" to minimize mess and make clean-up easy. Work from right to left (or whatever is comfortable for you), with bowls of cornmeal, buttermilk, and a second cornmeal. Have one "wet hand" and one "dry hand." This will prevent your fingers from getting sticky with batter.

T-Burg Sweet-Potato Fries

When I first moved to Trumansburg I met Eric and Mary Ott, owners of the legendary Rongovian Embassy. Over the counter of the original Simply Red, Eric shared his memories of Sweet Potato Fries on long-ago menus at the Rongo. On Eric's next visit I surprised him with a bowl of my fresh-cut fries and watched as a broad smile slowly crept across his face. Sweet Potato Fries were back in T-Burg! Since then, these staples of Southern cuisine have become standard fare on Monday nights.

Heat oil in a heavy bottom 1 gallon pot, or a pot that is at least twice the volume of the oil. Use a candy thermometer to monitor the temperature of the oil at 375-degrees. Drain the potatoes and dry with a paper towel. Once the oil has reached temperature, drop in fries, a small handful at a time until they are all added, taking care not to splash the hot oil. Fry for 10 minutes, until they float to the top, then use a pair of tongs to pull the fries out of the oil and place into a large metal mixing bowl. Toss the fries with herb mix, pile onto a platter and serve with the curry mayonnaise.

2 sweet potatoes, tips off, quartered, cut into ¼" strips

2 tablespoons herb mix (recipe p. 20)

1/2 cup curry mayonnaise (recipe p. 40)

4 cups vegetable oil or peanut oil for frying

Makes 4 servings.

MAMA SAYS...

If you want to establish your Southern cooking bona fides, Sweet Potato Fries is where to begin your quest. Start with plump, well-ripened potatoes, pile high and always serve with Curry Mayonnaise for dipping.

Homestyle Potato Chips

Here's an alternative to store-bought potato chips and a great way to impress party guests on Saturday night. Drizzled with thick, creamy blue cheese and sprinkled with parmesan, these chips are appetizing and addictive. The real secret of making crispy chips is using a mandolin-type slicer (or meat slicer) so you can slice the potatoes into strips of equal thickness. To earn extra points, serve alongside chardonnay from Sheldrake Point Vineyard.

For the cheese sauce:

2 cups heavy cream

1 cup blue cheese, crumbled

For the potato chips:

2 Yukon gold potatoes, peeled

2 tablespoons herb mix (recipe p. 20)

1/4 cup parmesan cheese, grated

1 tablespoon parsley, chopped

4 cups vegetable or peanut oil

In a small saucepan heat the heavy cream and blue cheese crumbles on low temperature. Whisk this mixture occasionally until reduced by one-third. Remove from heat and hold.

Using a mandolin set at 1/16th inch, slice potatoes. Place all slices in a large bowl of water. Allow to sit for at least 20 minutes. Heat oil in a heavy-bottom 1 gallon pot, or a pot that is at least twice the volume of the oil. Use a candy thermometer to monitor the temperature of the oil at 350-degrees. Drain the potatoes and dry with a paper towel (to prevent oil from spattering from the excess moisture). Once the oil has reached temperature, slowly add potato slices and fry for 10 minutes or until they float to the top. Use a pair of tongs to quickly remove the chips from the oil. Place on a sheet pan and allow to cool.

When ready to serve, toss with the herb mix, then spoon the blue cheese sauce over top. Sprinkle with the parmesan cheese and parsley.

Makes 4 servings.

MAMA SAYS...

Besides a topping for chips, the thick sauce is amazing on steamed broccoli, Brussels sprouts, and grilled chicken breast.

Garlic and Herb Fries

As good as they are plain, these fries really shine when tossed with herb mix and rich herb butter, a more soulful take on everyday McDonald's fries. Russet potatoes are starchy potatoes and after slicing should be soaked in cold water for 1 hour. Skipping this step may result in a "starchy" flavor and cause the fries to stick together.

Place all ingredients in a food processor with blade attachment and pulse until all ingredients are incorporated and evenly blended. Place mix into a small saucepan and heat on low until it has all melted.

Heat oil in a heavy-bottom 1 gallon pot (use a pot that is twice the volume of the oil). Use a candy thermometer to monitor the temperature of the oil at 350-degrees. Drain the potatoes (best when working in 2 batches) and dry with a paper towel. Once the oil has reached temperature, drop the fries in a small handful at a time until they are all added, taking care not to splash hot oil. Fry for 10 minutes until they float to the top then use a pair of tongs to pull the fries out of the oil. Place in a large metal mixing bowl. Toss with the herb mix, herb butter and additional salt to taste. Pile on a plate and serve with the aioli.

Makes 6 servings.

For the herb butter:

4 ounces butter at room temperature, cut into cubes

1 tablespoon garlic, chopped

1/4 cup parsley, chopped

1/4 cup cilantro, chopped

1/4 cup basil, chopped

3/4 teaspoon herb mix (recipe p. 20)

For the fries:

4 cups vegetable or peanut oil

3 russet potatoes, cut into long sticks one-quarter inch thick (keep covered in cold water)

2 tablespoons herb mix (recipe p. 20)

4 ounces garlic herb butter (recipe p. 45)

1 teaspoon salt

1/2 cup roasted garlic-lemon aioli (recipe p. 41)

MAMA SAYS...

In my homeland of South Africa we call them "slaap chips" (the pronunciation focuses on the "aa" sounds as in "aah"). In fish shops they come wrapped in paper. Then we load them with ketchup and malt vinegar.

Sweet Potato-Roasted Red Pepper Butternut Soup with Chipotle Pepper Cream

Autumn is a beautiful time in the Finger Lakes. The arrival of the first cool days is a wonderful time to just stay in the moment and feast on comfort food. At this time of the year my cooking turns to richer, more warming dishes, and when I found these seasonal foodstuffs in my pantry, I imagined a substantial soup, designed to fill both the heart and stomach. Its secret lies in the subtle kick from chipotle cream.

Toss butternut, sweet potato and red pepper together in a bowl with olive oil and herb mix. Spread on a cookie sheet and roast in a pre-heated oven for 45 minutes at 400-degrees. Heat the oil in a large pot. Add the onion, celery and garlic and sauté until translucent. Add the butternut, sweet potato and roasted red peppers. Add the saffron, cumin and stock and simmer on low for 1 ½ hours. Puree soup in a food processor or with a stick blender.

In a stand mixer (with the whip attachment) whip the cream cheese, yogurt and chipotle peppers until combined.

Serve soup in bowls and top with chipotle cream.

Makes 8 servings.

For the soup:
2 1/2 pounds butternut, seeded, peeled and cut into chunks
4 pounds of sweet potato, peeled and diced
2 cups of red peppers, sliced
1/4 cup olive oil
4 tablespoons herb mix (recipe p. 20)
2 cups white onion, diced
2 cups celery, diced
6 cloves garlic
1/4 cup olive oil
1 tablespoon saffron
2 tablespoons cumin powder
12 cups veggie or chicken stock

For the chipotle cream:
8 ounces cream cheese
1/4 cup yogurt, plain
2 tablespoons chipotle peppers, in adobo sauce
pinch salt, to taste
pinch pepper, to taste

MAMA SAYS...

Butternut squash is a common vegetable in my homeland of South Africa. It not only makes a very tasty soup, it's often cooked on a barbeque (or what we call a "braai", wrapped in foil with spices such as nutmeg and cinnamon.

Shrimp Bisque with Crème Fraiche and Shitake Mushrooms

Anyone who has seen the movie "Forrest Gump" knows there are many ways to prepare shrimp. For my taste, no preparation fills the mouth with the essence of savory shrimp quite like this luscious, aromatic soup. It's wonderfully satisfying as lunch with a salad or sandwich or as an elegant first course to dinner.

In a large pot, heat the oil over medium heat, add the shells and sauté until they are lightly toasted. Add onion, carrots, garlic and red pepper flakes and cook until translucent. Deglaze the pan with the white wine and add the remainder of the stock ingredients. Cook until reduced by half, strain and set aside.

In a large saucepan, melt the butter over medium heat. Add the flour and whisk until smooth. Cook until lightly toasted. Slowly whisk in the shrimp stock (to avoid lumps). Add the tomato puree. Split the vanilla bean and scrape the inside of the pod into the stock. Add cream, sherry, demi-glace and lavender and simmer for 30 minutes. Add the shrimp and season with salt and pepper. Top with crème fraiche and poached mushrooms and serve.

Makes 6 servings.

For the shrimp stock:

1/4 cup vegetable oil
2 pounds shrimp shells
2 cups white onion, peeled and diced
2 cups carrots, peeled and chopped
1 teaspoon garlic, chopped
1/2 teaspoon red pepper flakes
2 cups white wine
1 small can tomato puree
1 teaspoon herb mix (recipe p. 20)
4 bay leaves
5 peppercorns
4 quarts of water

For the bisque:

5 tablespoons butter
1/2 cup flour
3-1/3 cups shrimp stock
1 cup tomato puree
1 vanilla bean sliced and scraped of its seeds
2/3 cup heavy cream
1/2 cup dry cooking sherry
1/3 cup demi-glace
1 teaspoon fresh lavender, chopped fine
2 pounds of shrimp, peeled and deveined
3/4 cup crème fraiche
1-1/3 cup shiitake mushrooms, sliced and poached

MAMA SAYS...

The secret lies in extracting flavor from the shells. Toasting the raw shells concentrate their flavors before making the stock.

Hot Dixie Dip

This is a wonderfully creamy and tasty dip, made rich with crab-meat and artichokes, while capers add a subtle zest. Serve with crackers, toasted pita points, or slices of your favorite bread.

Place all ingredients in a large bowl and mix thoroughly (using only 1 cup of the parmesan cheese, reserving the balance to sprinkle on top of finished dip). Be sure the cream cheese is mixed in thoroughly.

Place the mixture into an oven-proof dish, add the additional parmesan, cover with foil and bake in a pre-heated oven for 30 minutes at 375-degrees. Serve with toasted pita points or slices of bread.

Makes 12 servings.

1 pound lump crabmeat

2 cups artichokes, quartered

1/2 cup celery, diced

1/2 cup white onion, diced

2 tablespoons capers

1 tablespoon herb mix (recipe p. 20)

juice of 1 lemon

1-1/2 cups parmesan cheese

1/2 cup bread crumbs

1/4 cup mayonnaise

8 ounces cream cheese

MAMA SAYS...

Here's how to warm up a party. Bring out the dip in a warmed serving dish just after guests have arrived, and let them know it's time to dig in.

Chicken Livers Peri-Peri

The hot sauce made from dried and soaked piri-piri chili peppers is called "African Red Devil." Although its origin is probably Portuguese, the fiery hot sauce has become a classic West African accompaniment to just about everything from eggs to steak. Make a bigger batch and store in the fridge to add to your next meal.

Heat olive oil in a sauté pan. Add the garlic and onions and sauté until the onions are translucent. Add the Roma tomatoes, red peppers and herb mix and continue to simmer on medium heat. Once the tomatoes have started to break down and the sauce has started to brown, squeeze in the lemon juice and turn off the sauce. Cool and store in an air-tight container until needed.

In a medium-size sauté pan, heat the butter and olive oil on medium heat.

Add in the chicken livers and allow to cook for 5 minutes. Turn and add in the herb mix and peri-peri sauce. Sauté an additional 5 minutes, then pull the pan from the heat and add in the sherry (take care if you are cooking on a gas stove since the sherry may ignite). Add the heavy cream and allow the sauce to reduce until the surface of the sauce has begun to bubble. Remove from heat, portion the livers into bowls, top with the sauce and serve.

Makes 4 servings.

For the peri-peri sauce:

1/3 cup olive oil

6 cloves of garlic, sliced

1 cup onion, diced

1-1/2 cups roma tomatoes, diced

1 tablespoons red pepper flakes

1 tablespoon herb mix (recipe p. 20)

juice of 1 lemon

For the chicken livers:

1 tablespoon butter

2 tablespoons olive oil

1 pound chicken livers

1 tablespoon herb mix (recipe p. 20)

1/2 cup peri-peri sauce

1/4 cup cooking sherry

1/2 cup heavy cream

MAMA SAYS...

Five years ago I returned to South Africa, and over dinner at a safari camp I was treated to this lovely dish of chicken livers with peri-peri sauce. I have embellished the original recipe, adding sherry and heavy cream. Enjoy with a loaf of crusty bread.

Sides

Buttermilk Mashed Potatoes

Mashed potatoes are one of my favorite foods, and I love trying all the variations. But no mashers beat the down-home goodness of sour buttermilk and creamy potatoes, a culinary tradition that stretches back to deep and very Southern roots. Whisked to a fare-thee-well, mine are anointed with lots of butter, sea salt, cracked pepper, and fresh chives.

Peel, cube and cover potatoes with the water and salt. Boil for 20 minutes, then drain when done. Mash the potatoes using a whisk. Shake off the whisk and incorporate the buttermilk, butter, ground pepper and chives. Taste and adjust the seasonings according to taste.

Makes 6 servings.

9 medium-size Yukon gold potatoes, peeled and cubed

2 tablespoons sea salt

1/2 cup buttermilk

4 tablespoons unsalted butter

1 tablespoon fresh ground black pepper

1/2 cup chopped fresh chives

water

MAMA SAYS...

The smooth, buttery taste of Yukon gold potatoes makes them the best choice for this recipe. I like this method because it makes a smooth mashed potato with only a small amount of lumps. Keep warm on the stove top or in the oven in a heat proof dish on low temp. And, if you're watching your weight, buttermilk mashed potatoes taste a lot like mashed potatoes made with heavy cream, but have far fewer calories.

Saturday Morning Supper Hash

Some dishes actually improve in flavor when prepared in advance. This hash is an example of one of those make-ahead sides. Roasting the potatoes first develops depth of flavor and sweetness, eliminating the need to add any sugar that is often required in sweet potato dishes. Bacon enriches the hash without taking over.

Roast the sweet potatoes in a 400-degree oven for 40 minutes. Cool, peel and cut into chunks. Coat the bacon with the Cajun spice and roast in the oven for 15 minutes at 350-degrees, allow to cool, then dice the bacon. Heat a pan, add the olive oil, then the onions and sauté for 10 minutes, until translucent. Add the red peppers and bacon. Sauté for 5 minutes, then add the diced sweet potatoes and cook until the potatoes are heated through and a little crispy. Scoop into an oven-proof dish and serve.

1/4 cup olive oil

4 sweet potatoes

1-1/2 cups white onion, sliced thin

2 cups red peppers, sliced thin

1/2 pound bacon

1/4 cup Cajun spice (recipe p. 22)

Makes 8 servings.

MAMA SAYS...

Hash works for breakfast or brunch or as a side dish with dinner. Serve poached eggs on a bed of this spicy sweet potato hash. (Chilling the potatoes in the refrigerator prevents them from falling apart when they are sautéed).

Truck-Stop Barbeque Beans

Start by brewing up a rich, strong cuppa joe. Coffee adds a deep, smoky body to barbeque dishes, and coffee-spiked baked beans is a popular dish in truck-stops and diners across the South. There's nothing subtle about these smoky, slow-cooked beans, served either hot or cold. I use cane sugar as a sweetener and molasses for the beautiful mahogany color it imparts.

Mix all ingredients together in a bowl. Pour into an oven-proof pan and cover with foil. Bake in 400-degree oven for 1-1/2 hours. Uncover and serve.

Makes 6 servings.

1-1/2 cups pinto beans, drained and rinsed

1-1/2 cups kidney beans, drained and rinsed

3 ounces barbeque sauce (recipe p. 43)

1 cups onions, finely-diced

1/2 cup strong coffee

1-1/2 tablespoon barbeque spice (recipe p. 21)

2 tablespoons molasses

1/4 cup cane sugar

MAMA SAYS...

Variety is the spice of baked beans. I favor this mix of pinto and kidney beans, but the recipe works with everything from limas to navy beans. The recipe can be spiced up by adding thick slab cut bacon to it as you cook it to add more depth to its flavor.

Okra and Tomatoes

The classic Southern courtship of okra and tomatoes mingles the characteristic gummy juices with sweet-sour flavors into a silky, rich broth as they stew together and smother together.

In a small pot, sauté the onions and oil until translucent. Add the okra, tomatoes and herbs. Simmer on low for 30 minutes and serve.

Makes 6 servings.

1-1/2 cups diced white onion

1/4 cup olive oil

2-14.5 ounce cans diced tomatoes and juice

16 ounces frozen bag of okra

1 tablespoon herb mix (recipe p. 20)

MAMA SAYS...

Fresh tomatoes can be substituted for canned, but the okra is better if frozen. Fresh garden-picked okra can be rinsed, sliced into ½ thick pieces and then frozen. I place them on a cookie sheet covered in plastic to freeze them individually and then place them in a zip lock bag to keep until needed.

Sweet Corn on the Cob

Sweet corn, dripping with butter, is a purely American passion. It's a sure sign of summer and a compliment to nearly all barbecued dishes. Leftover corn can be cut off the cob and sprinkled over a green salad.

Preheat oven to 400-degrees or fire up the grill. In a mixing bowl mix together the butter, chili powder, lime juice and salt. Place each ear of corn on a piece of heavy duty aluminum foil. Slather 3 teaspoons of the butter mixture onto each ear of corn. Wrap the corn up in the foil, pulling both sides of the foil up towards the center of the cob and rolling the foil over so as to present a little package that won't allow the butter to run out of the sides. Place the cobs in an oven-proof dish and bake in the oven for 25 minutes or on the grill for 20 minutes, rotatating the corn from side to side to even out the cooking. Serve with extra butter on the side.

4 ears of corn

1 stick of unsalted butter at room temperature

1 teaspoon chili powder

juice of one lime

pinch of salt

Makes 4 servings.

MAMA SAYS...

If there is a downside to corn on the cob, it's the fact that the sugar in corn begins to turn to starch the instant it is cut from the stalk. Find your nearest local farm stand and keep the elapsed time from stalk to grill as short as possible.

Hoppin' John

Legend has it that a Georgia landowner's one-legged slave, John, hopped around the table as he served a meal of rice and black-eyed peas. The meal was so well liked that it was named after him.

In a small pot, cook the black eyed peas, rice, water and salt on medium high for 30-45 minutes. (The beans should be soft enough to squish but still have a little texture to them). Drain the beans and rinse quickly. Place in a mixing bowl and add in the curry spice, soy sauce and parsley. Put the bean mixture into an oven-proof dish, and add 1/2 cup of water. Cover and bake in a 350-degree oven for 20 minutes. Remove from the oven and serve.

Makes 6 servings.

1 cup black eyed peas

1/2 cup wild rice

8 cups water

1 tablespoon salt

1 tablespoon curry spice blend (recipe p. 23)

1/4 cup soy sauce

1/2 bunch Italian flat leaf parsley

MAMA SAYS...

Black-eyed peas are a Southern tradition for New Year's Day. The more you eat on that day, the more prosperous you will be in the coming year. On the day after New Year's Day, leftover Hoppin' John is called Skippin' Jenny, and further demonstrates one's frugality, hopefully bringing an even better chance of prosperity in the New Year.

Roasted Root Vegetables

This dish is intoxicatingly aromatic, with the scent of the roasting herbs releasing their essence into these winter staples. Roasted to sweet tenderness, they make a warming accompaniment to Country Fried Steak.

Toss all ingredients in a bowl and place in a covered oven-proof dish for 1-1/2 hours at 375-degrees. (The vegetables will caramelize slightly when done). Toss with parsley and serve.

Makes 6 servings.

1/4 cup shallots, peeled and sliced

2 tablespoons garlic cloves, sliced

1 cup rutabaga, peeled and diced into half-inch pieces

1 cup parsnips, peeled and sliced into half-inch pieces

1 cup turnips, peeled and sliced into half-inch pieces

1/4 cup olive oil

1 tablespoon herb mix (recipe p. 20)

2 tablespoons chopped parsley

MAMA SAYS...

It's like a family reunion from the root vegetable garden, the combination determined by whatever is in season.

Cajun Butter

Cajun seasoning mix provides the spicy, smoky punch to my base butter, and Worcestershire adds mellow richness. Killer Shrimp, Jambalaya, and Shrimp and Grits deserve no less. What you get is a uniquely complex, intense, but not overly spicy dish.

In a stand mixer with whipping attachment, place the garlic, Cajun spice and Worcestershire sauce, and mix until well combined. Add the butter into the mixer one chunk at a time. (Do not add the next cube of butter until the first one has incorporated well). Keep adding the butter until it is all added in. Continue to mix for a few minutes more. Scrape out and store in an air tight container in the fridge.

1 pound of butter at room temperature, cut into chunks

1/4 cup Cajun spice (recipe on p. 22)

1/4 cup garlic, sliced thin

2 tablespoons Worcestershire sauce

Makes 3 cups.

MAMA SAYS...

Bored with plain-butter corn on the cob? Try slathering this butter on grilled sweet corn for a surprising kick.

Collard Greens with Ham Hock

Collards need to simmer slowly with a piece of ham hock (the end of a smoked ham where the foot was attached to the hog's leg) to temper the tough texture and smoothe out the bitter flavor. Traditionally, collards are served with freshly-baked corn bread to dip into the "pot-likker," the concentrated broth left after the long boil of the greens.

Place the ham hock and the salt into the pot first, then add the collards and water. Cover with foil and allow to simmer for up to 3 hours on low temperature. Drain, discard the ham hock and serve.

Makes 6 servings.

1 ham hock

2 tablespoons salt

3 heads collard greens, sliced half-inch thick, down to where the stem thickens

12 cups water

MAMA SAYS...

Collards become sweeter after the first frost, so to simulate this in the restaurant we freeze the greens in the walk-in cooler, then cut them while they are still frozen. I prefer them plain, just accented by the smokiness of the ham hock and a bit of salt. But you may add pepper vinegar (recipe p. 56) or honey butter (recipe p. 44) to your "mess o' greens."

Fragrant Basmati Rice

Basmati is a naturally-fragrant, long-grained rice from India, grown at the foothills of the Himalayas. The color is provided by turmeric powder, a member of the ginger family known for its warm and peppery flavor.

Place all ingredients in a heat-proof dish. Bake in a pre-heated oven at 350-degrees for 30 minutes.

Makes 6 servings.

> 1-1/2 cups basmati rice
>
> 3 cups water
>
> 1-1/2 teaspoons turmeric
>
> 1/4 cup raisins
>
> 1-/2 teaspoons salt
>
> pinch of saffron

MAMA SAYS...

Time this out to be ready at the same time you want to serve an accompanying curry dish.

Wild Rice

Very much an autumn treat, the distinctive nutty flavor and texture of wild rice combines with the wholesomeness of brown rice for a de-lovely side dish that looks as good as it tastes. It can be prepared ahead of time, refrigerated and popped into the microwave for reheating just before serving.

Place the brown rice, wild rice, water and salt into an oven-proof dish. Cover with foil and bake in a pre-heated oven for 20 minutes at 375-degrees. Remove from the oven and keep covered until ready to serve.

1 cup brown rice

1/2 cup wild rice

3 cups water

2 teaspoons salt

Makes 6 servings.

MAMA SAYS...

I like to spoon 2 tablespoons of garlic herb butter over the top just before I serve this dish, along with a couple of lemon wedges.

Classics

Honey-Stung Fried Chicken

It's the dish that's near and dear to the hearts (and stomachs) of the Monday night crowd. We add honey butter and drizzled honey to the chicken when it comes out of the hot oil, served up with our own wine country version of hospitality. Be sure to make enough for dinner and still have a few pieces leftover. It's even better cold the next day.

Whisk all ingredients for the marinade together in a metal bowl. Place the chicken pieces skin side down into the bowl and allow to marinade 3 to 12 hours in the fridge. Heat the peanut oil to 350-degrees in a large cast-iron pan. Dredge the chicken in the flour coating and shake off the excess. Place the dark pieces first into the oil, allow them 5 minutes to cook, then place the breast pieces into the oil and continue to cook for 15 more minutes. Monitor the oil temperature throughout cooking, starting out on high temp, then turning down to medium. Pull out a piece of the dark meat towards the end of the 15-minutes and stick a meat thermometer into the center of the chicken. It should reach 180-degrees. If done, remove all pieces and allow to cool slightly on a paper towel. Place chicken pieces onto a plate and top with honey and honey butter.

Makes 4 servings.

1 whole chicken (organic, free-range preferred), cut into quarters

8 cups peanut oil

For the marinade:

2 cups of buttermilk

2 teaspoons salt

1 teaspoon ground black pepper

1 tablespoon hot sauce

1 tablespoon smoked chipotle peppers in adobo sauce

For the coating:

1-1/2 cups flour

1 teaspoon salt

1/2 teaspoon ground black pepper

4 tablespoons honey butter

4 ounces honey

MAMA SAYS...

Please take care – the oil is VERY hot. Use a candy thermometer to monitor the overall temperature. The pot size that you use should allow the oil to cover the chicken entirely.

Family Reunion Dinner Ham

It may seem redundant to boil this ham in a spiced bath after it's been cured and smoked, but it really makes an impact on its overall character and flavor. Papa Gary says it's the best ham he's ever had. This makes a succulent holiday ham, then as leftovers for sandwiches or grilled and served with eggs for breakfast. The glaze adds depth to the ham's flavor and gloss to the appearance--just the right finishing touch.

Unwrap the ham from its plastic seal and place in a large pot, leave the netting on the ham (as it makes it easier to turn while boiling). Toss in all the other ingredients. On medium heat, allow to simmer for 2 hours, turning the ham every hour. Remove from pot, drain, and cut off the netting. Score the outside fat in criss-crosses and press a whole clove into the center of the diamond shapes. Place onto a heat-proof tray. (Place foil under it so that the tray is easier to clean).

Heat the glaze once the ham has come out of the broth. Spoon 1/3 of the glaze over the ham, and place under the broiler until the fat starts to crackle.

Glaze again a second time and place under the broiler (take care not to burn). Remove from the oven and place on a carving board. Slice and serve.

For the ham:
1 6-7 pound picnic shoulder ham (bone-in)
1 gallon water
1 bottle of red wine
4 bay leaves
2 cinnamon sticks
1 tablespoon cardamom seeds
1 tablespoon whole cloves

For the glaze:
12 ounces red currant jam
1 ½ teaspoons ground cinnamon
1 ½ teaspoons smoked paprika
1 tablespoon red wine vinegar

Makes 8 servings.

Leftover ham can be stored in the refrigerator for up to 3 days. For longer storage, you can freeze the ham and store it up to 2 months.

Damn Good Barbeque Ribs

"Country style ribs" refers to the cut of meat, not the manner of preparation. There are three types of ribs--spare ribs which come from the belly, baby back which come from the loin, and "country style" which are not actually ribs and are cut from the blade end of the loin. Country style ribs have by far and away much more meat and very little if any bone, and it's the extra marbling and meat that allows them to cook so long. These ribs are just the ticket for those who prefer to use a knife or fork.

Place barbeque spice in a bowl. Liberally cover the ribs with the spice and place into a 1 to 2 inch-deep roasting pan standing up on their sides. Pour in the cider vinegar. Cover with foil and roast in a pre-heated oven for 2 to 2-1/2 hours at 375-degrees. (The meat should squish easily between your fingers at two hours. If not, continue roasting for an additional half hour). Pull the pan

> 4 ½ to 5 pounds of pork loin country-style ribs
>
> 4 cups of cider vinegar
>
> 1/4 cup barbeque spice (recipe p. 21)
>
> 1 cup barbeque sauce (recipe p. 43)

out of the oven, remove the foil, and drain off the vinegar. Brush top side of ribs with barbeque sauce; return to oven, and broil until bubbling. Turn ribs over, brush with barbeque sauce, and continue broiling until bubbling. Serve 2 ribs per serving.

Makes 6 servings.

MAMA SAYS...

Pair these bold ribs with Mac and Cheese and Collard Greens, and finish it all with a nap.

Blue Plate Special Meatloaf

Hope springs eternal in the quest for the perfect meatloaf, and this may be close to perfection. The array of vegetables adds moisture to this mixture, and not only does it result in a juicier loaf, but also provides lots of extra flavor and aroma. The addition of savory spice and herb mixes make this down-home dish anything but ordinary. Comfort-foodies will enjoy it beside a heaping pile of buttery mashed potatoes.

Step 1: place ground beef into a mixing bowl. Add remaining ingredients into a food processor with the blade attachment and pulse a few times, then add to the ground beef.

Step 2: add these ingredients to the meatloaf mix, setting aside 4-ounces of the barbeque sauce for the top of the meatloaf. Using your hands, combine until all the ingredients have been incorporated. Place a piece of aluminum foil onto a cookie sheet tray. Spray with non-stick spray. Form the meatloaf mix into a firm loaf. Top with the reserved barbeque sauce. Place in a pre-heated oven for 45 minutes at 350-degrees for one hour or until the center temperature comes out at 160-degrees. Cool slightly, slice and serve.

Makes 8 servings.

Ingredients for Step 1:

2-1/2 pounds ground beef (full fat)

1 cup white onion cut into chunks

3 garlic cloves

1 cup celery sliced

1 cup carrots peeled and sliced

Ingredients for Step 2:

2 eggs

2 tablespoons barbeque spice

1 tablespoon herb mix

8 ounces barbeque sauce

2 cups breadcrumbs

MAMA SAYS...

I prefer to bake my meatloaf one day ahead, let it cool it over night, then, using a serrated knife, cut into ½ inch slices, brush with barbeque sauce and reheat in a 375- degree oven for 10 minutes. As leftovers, it makes great sandwiches.

Cajun Cornmeal-Crusted Catfish

Farmed-raised catfish has a mild, slightly sweet flavor that soars with the addition of Cajun spices, and its firm texture is complimented by the snap of cornmeal crust. Here's a dish that never fails to elicit whoops and hollers from the Monday night regulars.

4 catfish fillets

1 cup cornmeal

1 tablespoon Cajun spice (recipe p. 22)

2 tablespoons olive oil

2 tablespoons butter

12 ounces Cajun remoulade (recipe p. 39)

Mix the cornmeal and the Cajun spice. When looking at the catfish you will notice that it has a raised side and a flat side. Place the flat side down into the cornmeal and shake to fully cover the fish. Remove from the cornmeal and place on a baking sheet, repeating for the other three fish. Place 2 cast-iron sauté pans on a medium-high heat (the pans need to have handles that can go into the oven). Add 1 tablespoon of olive oil and butter to each of 2 pans. Once pans are heated and the butter has melted, lay the catfish raised side down into the butter and oil and sauté for 3 minutes. Using a pair of tongs, flip over each fish and place into a pre-heated oven for 15 minutes at 375-degrees. Use a flat metal spatula to remove the fish from the pans and onto dinner plates. Top each fillet with 3 ounces of remoulade.

Makes 4 servings.

MAMA SAYS...

Always serve this preparation with a robust remoulade, beer, coleslaw, beer, french fries, beer, and of course, beer.

Creole Jambalaya

Jambalaya originated in the French Quarter of New Orleans as a New World version of Spanish paella, with spices from the Caribbean providing a unique identity. The dish has evolved along a variety of different lines. Creole Jambalaya includes tomatoes, whereas Cajun Jambalaya is tomato-less.

For the rice:

Place the brown rice, wild rice, water and salt into an oven proof dish. Cover with foil and bake in the pre-heated oven for 20 minutes at 400-degrees. Pull out of the oven and keep covered on the counter until ready to prepare the jambalaya.

For the jambalaya:

Place a large wide pot on medium high heat, add the Cajun butter and allow the butter to melt. Add the shallots, chorizo and tomatoes. Sauté until the shallots are translucent. Add the seafood, rice, clam juice, white wine and herbs. Stir and place in the oven to bake for 15 minutes. Scoop into large bowls and serve.

Makes 6 servings.

For the rice:
1/4 cup brown rice
1/4 cup wild rice
1-1/2 cups water
1 tsp salt

For the jambalaya:
5 tablespoons Cajun butter (recipe p. 80)
1 cup sliced shallots
3 Roma tomatoes diced small
1 link of cooked chorizo sausage cut into 8 pieces
1 pound white fish cut into 1 inch pieces
6 jumbo size scallops
6 large shrimp, no shells
1 pound fresh mussels
2 tablespoons herb mix (recipe p. 20)
2 cups clam juice
1 cup white wine
1-1/2 cups wild rice mix

MAMA SAYS...

This recipe is smoky, spicy and rich, yet not so spicy that you'll need a pitcher of milk to douse the flames in your mouth. I like to serve it with a side of cornbread and honey butter.

True Shrimp and Grits

This dish started out as a humble breakfast for Southern coastal fishermen and their families, especially during shrimp season (May through December). Originally called "breakfast shrimp," the dish consisted of a pot of grits along with shrimp cooked in a little bacon grease or butter. Not just for breakfast anymore, this dressed-up version has a place at brunch, lunch, or dinner.

For the grits: in a small pot, heat the water to a rolling boil. Add the salt and grits and lower heat to a simmer. Whisk until the grits have thickened, about 3-5 minutes. Add the cheddar cheese. Pour out and flatten with a spatula onto a cookie sheet. Portion four ways and reheat in a 350-degree oven for 10 minutes as the sauce is being prepared. Dish into four large bowls. (Can be made ahead and kept in the fridge until ready to serve with the sauce).

For the shrimp: in a large flat bottom pot, heat the olive oil on medium heat and add the Cajun butter. Add the zucchini, summer squash, red peppers, red onions and chorizo and sauté for 5 minutes. Add the shrimp and deglaze the pan with the sherry. (Remove the pan from the heat when you add the sherry as it may ignite a small amount of flame). Add the cream and continue to cook until it has reached a rolling boil. Once the shrimp has become opaque remove from pan and set aside as the sauce reduces. Spoon the shrimp and equal portions of the sauce over the grits.

Make 4 servings.

For the grits:

1/2 cup quick cooking grits

2 cups cold water

1 teaspoon salt

1 cup cheddar cheese, grated

For the shrimp:

1/4 cup olive oil

4 tablespoons Cajun butter (recipe p. 80)

1 zucchini, cut into half moon slices

1 summer squash, cut into half moon slices

1/2 cup red pepper, sliced

1/2 cup red onion, sliced

16 (13-15 count) peeled and deveined shrimp

1 chorizo sausage cut into 8 smaller pieces

3 ounces sherry

9 ounces heavy cream

MAMA SAYS...

I make my grits on the stiff side to make sopping-up of the rich, spicy and creamy sauce just a bit easier. Enjoy with a glass of Sheldrake Point Vineyard Riesling

Boardwalk Crab Cakes
with Lemon-Caper-Garlic Aioli

Crab cakes with Southern roots are flavored with the "holy trinity" of Cajun cooking--onion, bell pepper, and celery--then pan-fried to a golden brown. Serve these crispy, creamy cakes with a tall stack of hushpuppies.

For the aioli:

In a kitchen aid mixer, blend all the ingredients until thoroughly combined. Store in fridge until needed.

For the crab cakes:

Heat olive oil in a heavy sauté pan. Add the peppers, celery, red onion and jalapeno and sauté for 5 minutes. In a mixing bowl, combine the crab meat, egg, 1-1/3 cups plain breadcrumbs, salt, mayo and sauté veggies. Mix thoroughly with your hands until well combined. Refrigerate the crab mix for an hour. In a sauté pan, heat 1 cup of olive oil. Form the crab cakes into half-inch thick cakes, using 1/2 cup crabmeat for each. Coat with breadcrumb mix. Sauté 4 minutes per side, until they are golden brown. Top with aioli and serve.

Makes 8 servings.

For the aioli:

1 cup mayonnaise

2 teaspoons herb mix (recipe p. 20)

1 tablespoon lemon juice

2 cloves garlic

2 tablespoons capers

For the crab cakes:

3 tablespoons olive oil

1/3 cup red bell pepper, diced

1/3 cup celery, diced

1/3 cup red onion, diced

1 jalapeno pepper, diced

1 pound crab meat, claw and lump

1 large egg, beaten to blend

4 cups plain breadcrumbs

1 teaspoon salt

1/2 cup mayonnaise

Mix the alliance of ingredients together gently – the idea is to keep the crabmeat as lumpy as possible so it will hold up during the cooking process. Great as an appetizer or topped with a poached egg and hollandaise for a "Gulf Coast" brunch.

Honest-to-Goodness Chicken Pot Pie

There are foods that make you feel good. This savory pie filled with sweet, creamy chicken stew is the very definition of "comfort food," the sort of dish you might imagine June Cleaver serving Ward, Wally and the Beaver.

For the chicken stew: place chicken in an oven proof dish. Sprinkle with salt and pepper. Add the chicken base, white wine and onions. Cover with foil and roast for 1-1/2 hours in a 375-degree oven. Allow to cool on the counter, strip the chicken from the bones and place the meat in a large baking dish. Return the bones to the stock in a pan and simmer for 15 minutes. Strain and set aside.

For the sauce: heat a small saucepan; add the butter and bacon and sauté 5 minutes. Whisk in the flour, stock and milk and simmer a few minutes. Add the mustard, parsley and thyme and allow to thicken. Pour over the chicken in the baking dish.

For the crust: in a small metal bowl, add the flour, cream of tartar and salt. Grate in the butter, then use fingers to combine the flour and butter until small pea-like balls form. Add the soda water and use a knife to mix the dough until it just comes together. Place in the fridge for 1 hour. Turn out, roll and cut into 8 disks to cover the pies. Place on a cookie sheet in the oven and bake for 20 to 30 minutes, until the filling bubbles and the crust is golden brown.

Makes 8 servings.

For the chicken stew:
2 chickens (3-pound average)
1 teaspoon salt
1/2 teaspoon ground black pepper
1 tablespoon chicken base
    with 2 cups of water
2 cups white wine
2 onions, peeled and
    quartered

For the sauce:
5 ounces butter
1/4 cup flour
1 cup strained chicken stock
3 cups whole milk
4 strips bacon
1 teaspoon mustard powder
1/4 cup chopped parsley
1 teaspoon dried thyme

For the crust:
1-1/2 cups flour
3/4 teaspoon cream of tartar
1/2 teaspoon salt
1/2 pound butter
1/2 cup soda water

MAMA SAYS...

My recipe makes 8 individual ramekins (I use ones that are 10 ounces deep in volume) or one 10-inch pie, both at least 2-inches deep.

Chicken-Fried Steak and Vidalia Onion Gravy

It's a steak prepared in the same manner as Southern fried chicken. That is to say it's breaded, fried in a cast iron skillet until crisp, then slathered in gravy. There's hardly a dish more satisfying when the weather is cold outside than a crunchy fried steak smothered in gravy and served with collards and fresh-baked biscuits for dipping in the gravy. The sweet flavor of Vidalia onions accents this light gravy.

For the gravy: in a sauté pan, heat the oil and butter add the onions and cook until they are translucent. Sprinkle with flour and mix in thoroughly. Whisk in the water and gravy master and cook for a few minutes, until it has thickened. Season with salt and pepper to taste. Turn off and hold until ready to serve.

For the steaks: in a mixing bowl, whisk the buttermilk, 2 teaspoons of salt and 1 teaspoon of black pepper. Marinate the steaks for at least 2 hours in the buttermilk mixture. In another mixing bowl, mix together the flour and the remaining salt and pepper. In a cast iron skillet, heat the oil on medium heat. Remove the steak from the buttermilk mixture. Dredge each steak in the flour, then the buttermilk, then back in the flour. Place each steak in the hot oil and fry for three minutes on one side, turn and fry 3 minutes. Remove from the pan, top with the Vidalia onion gravy and serve.

Makes 6 servings.

For the gravy:

1/4 cup vegetable oil

2 tablespoons butter

1-1/4 cups of Vidalia onions, sliced thin

2 tablespoons flour

1 cup water

1 cap of gravy master

Salt and pepper to taste

For the steaks:

2 cups of buttermilk

3 teaspoons salt

1-1/2 teaspoons ground black pepper

6 (4 oz.) pieces of cube steak (from the butcher this is sirloin steak that has been run a machine called a cuber which tenderizes the meat)

1-1/2 cups flour

1/2 cup vegetable oil

MAMA SAYS...

This recipe also works well for venison (first soak meat in the buttermilk to remove the gamey taste).

Specialties

Killer Shrimp

Jumbo shrimp are nestled in the rich, divine broth, spiked with local beer and a "killer" concoction of garlic and Cajun spices. Keep lots of napkins nearby as you peel shells off the shrimp, swirl them in the brew and devour, along with slices of baguette to mop up all the goodness. Not for the faint of palate!

Heat a skillet on the stove on medium-high heat. Add Cajun butter and allow to melt (take care not to burn). Add the shrimp, allow to cook for a minute or two, until the shrimp turn pink, then turn them over and allow them to cook another minute or two. Cover with the beer and clam juice, allowing the broth to bubble slightly. Serve in a giant bowl with two spoons and lots of bread for sopping up the sauce.

Makes 2 servings.

12 Jumbo (13/15 count) shrimp, shell on

4 ounces Cajun butter (recipe p. 80)

1 cup Ithaca Nut Brown ale

1 cup clam juice

1/2 baguette, cut into slices

MAMA SAYS...

I run a paring knife up the back of the shell to make peeling easier and to allow more of the flavorful broth inside. Be careful not to overcook the shrimp or burn the butter. It will leave an unpleasant taste in your mouth.

Mac-and-Cheese Deluxe

I like to take old-time recipes and make a few changes before bringing them back to the table with a twist. If you have deep nostalgia for cafeteria steam-table macaroni and cheese, you may be surprised by this grown-up version of the childhood prototype. For my make-over of the comforting, easygoing eats, I've substituted some fancy-pants ingredients while still upholding the virtues of the original concept.

For the sauce:

In a heavy bottom pot on medium heat, melt the butter and oil. Add the onion, garlic and shallots and sauté until translucent. Add the nutmeg, herb mix and flour and sauté for a couple minutes. Slowly whisk in the milk so as not to form lumps. Once incorporated, allow the milk to warm up, then whisk in the cheese and cook an additional 5 minutes, until all the cheese has melted. Turn off and allow to cool.

For the pasta:

Heat water to a boil, add the salt and oil, then the pasta. Set a timer for 6 minutes and cook until "al dente." Drain the pasta (don't rinse). Add the cheese sauce and place into an oven proof dish. Top with the cheddar and parmesan cheese and place in a pre-heated oven for 20 minutes at 350-degrees. Scoop and serve.

Makes 12 servings.

For the sauce:
- 4 tablespoons butter
- 1 tablespoon oil
- 1 cup white onion diced small
- 1 tablespoon garlic chopped small
- 1 tablespoon shallots chopped small
- 1/4 teaspoon nutmeg
- 1-1/2 tablespoon herb mix (recipe p. 20)
- 1/4 cup flour
- 4 cups whole milk
- 2-1/2 cups parmesan/asiago cheese blend

For the pasta:
- 1 pound dry noodles (penne or small pasta shells)
- 1 gallon water
- 1/4 cup salt
- 1/4 cup olive oil
- 2 cups cheddar cheese, grated
- 1/4 cup parmesan cheese, grated

Try topping with leftover crumbled cornbread or biscuits for a golden brown and crispy crust.

Veggie Cheeseburger with Barbeque Sauce

Veggie burgers were a staple in our house--my mom started making them when my sister Kadi decided to become a vegan. But all veggie burgers are not created equal, and I think you'll enjoy this savory, easy-to-prepare version. Serve with whole wheat buns or unadorned over a salad.

Place burger mix ingredients in a pot and boil 20 minutes (the lentils will be soft, the rice slightly firm). Drain and rinse.

While the lentils are cooking, place the celery, onion and carrots in a food processor and pulse into small pieces. Place into a large mixing bowl. Add rest of ingredients to the celery, carrot, onion mix. Add the lentil bean burger mix while still warm. Using your hands, mix well, until well combined and all ingredients are well incorporated. Allow to cool in the fridge at least 6 hours.

Cooking technique: form by hand into pattys, measured either ¾ cup or 6 ounces by weight. Heat a non-stick pan with a little oil on medium-high. Place burger in the pan, taking care so as not to splash the oil. Cook for 3 minutes on one side, turn over with a spatula and cook on the other side for another 3 minutes. Place in preheated 350-degree oven for 8 minutes. Remove from the oven, top with barbeque sauce and cheddar and place back in the oven for an additional two minutes. Serve on the whole wheat bun with the roasted garlic-lemon aioli.

Makes 10 servings.

Ingredients for burger mix:
1 cup French lentils
1/2 cup brown rice
1/4 cup wild rice
2 teaspoons salt
8 cups cold water
Remaining ingredients:
1/2 cup celery sliced
1/2 cup white onion diced
1/2 cup carrot, peeled and sliced thin
1 15-ounce can corn
1 15-ounce can black beans, drained and rinsed
1/4 cup chopped cilantro
1/4 cup Tahini
1 cup quick cooking oats
1 tablespoon herb mix
1 teaspoon salt
To serve, per burger:
10 whole wheat buns
1-1/2 cups barbeque sauce (recipe on p. 43)
2 cups cheddar cheese, grated
1-1/2 cups roasted garlic-lemon aioli (recipe p. 41)

MAMA SAYS...

If you let the burger mix cool overnight, it's easier to work with. For best results, take care not to overcook. For a make-ahead batch, just sear the burgers, then freeze.

"Where's the Beef" Chili

Break out your soup pot and fix up a batch of a vegetarian chili that sings with flavor. My recipe is a wonderful alternative to traditional chili, spiked with dark beer (Ithaca Nut Brown preferred), intended to satisfy the heartiest of appetites. You may adjust the measure of chipotle peppers to achieve desired "heat." Serve with cornbread (recipe p. 27) and Honey Butter (recipe p. 44).

In a medium size pot, heat the olive oil. Add the carrots, celery, onions and garlic and sauté until the onions are translucent. Add the cilantro, spices, beer, molasses, honey, coffee and chipotles. Stir the pot for a few minutes, then add in the water, beans and tomatoes. Simmer for 1-1/2 to 2 hours.

Makes 10 to 12 servings.

4 tablespoons oil

1-1/2 cups carrots peeled and sliced into quarter-inch chunks

1½ cups celery sliced

1 cup white onion cut into quarter-inch chunks

4 cloves garlic, peeled and sliced

1/2 bunch cilantro roughly chopped

1 tablespoon herb mix (recipe p. 20)

1 tablespoon barbeque spice mix (recipe p. 21)

1 dark beer

1/2 cup black strap molasses

1/4 cup honey

1/2 cup coffee

1 tablespoon smoked chipotle peppers in adobe sauce

4 cups kidney beans

4 cups pinto Beans

3 cups Roma tomatoes, diced

4 cups water

MAMA SAYS... Papa Gary uses the leftover chili to make layered nachos at home. A little cheddar cheese, chili, jalapenos, sour cream, and guacamole (along with a few Ithaca Pale Ales) make this a standard Sunday night meal for us.

Fearless Lemon-Garlic-Red Pepper Chicken

Red pepper flakes intensify the spicy heat in the marinade, an awesome flavor-enhancer for chicken, on the grill or oven-roasted. In either case, it deserves to be washed down with a glass of our local Sheldrake Point Vineyard Pinot Gris. To begin, place chicken and marinade in a 1-gallon Ziploc bag, then rotate the bag several times to insure the meat is thoroughly covered. Place the bag into the refrigerator for at least 3 hours.

Whisk garlic, olive oil, lemon juice, red pepper flakes, herb mix and sea salt together. Combine with chicken in Ziploc bag and marinate for 3 hours. Remove chicken from bag and place in an oven-proof roasting dish, skin side up. Spread leftover marinade liquid on the chicken breast before roasting. Cover with foil and roast in a pre-heated oven for 1 hour at 375-degrees. Uncover and roast an additional 20 minutes.

1 whole 3-4 lb. organic chicken, split down the middle

1/2 cup garlic cloves chopped

1/2 cup olive oil

1/2 cup fresh lemon juice

1 tablespoon red pepper flakes

1 tablespoon herb mix (recipe p. 20)

1 tablespoon sea salt

Chicken should temp out at 180-degrees when completely done.

Makes 4 servings.

MAMA SAYS...

If you'd like to tone down the heat, reduce the amount of red pepper flakes according to your own taste. Serve the roasted chicken on a platter with any assortment of side dishes – collard greens and black eyed peas are my personal favorites.

Grandma Willie's Chicken Pie

This is my South African grandma's meat pie recipe, lovingly prepared with chicken, bacon, white wine, and a flaky pastry. In South Africa, these savory pies are made without vegetables, unlike traditional "pot pies."

For the filling: place chicken, onion, bacon, water, wine, and spices (which should be placed in a cheese cloth and wrapped with a rubber band) in an oven proof dish. Cover with foil and roast 1-1/2 hours. Allow to cool and then strip the chicken from the bones. Drain stock from dish and place in a small pot. Return the chicken to the stock in a small pot; add the sago, vermicelli, lemon and egg. Return to heat and simmer for 10 minutes until thickened. (The noodles and tapioca will be soft but still uncooked). Scoop into 8 ramekins, top with crust and bake.

For the crust: in a small metal bowl, add the flour, cream of tartar and salt. Grate in the butter and then use fingers to combine the flour and butter until small pea like balls form. Add the soda water and use a knife to mix the dough until it just comes together. Place in the fridge for 1 hour. Turn out, roll and cut into 8 disks to cover the pies. Place on a cookie sheet in the oven and bake for 20-30 minutes at 375-degrees until the filling bubbles and the crust is golden brown.

Makes 8 servings.

For the filling:

1 chicken 3-4 pound average

1 onion peeled and quartered

4 strips of bacon cut into chunks

4 cups water

1 cup white wine

1 teaspoon each salt and ground pepper

1 teaspoon mace

1 teaspoon allspice

5 whole cloves

3 tablespoons Sago (small tapioca)

1/3 cup vermicelli noodles

juice of 1 lemon

1 egg beaten

For the crust:

1-1/2 cups flour

3/4 teaspoon cream of tartar

1/2 teaspoon salt

1/2 pound butter

1/2 cup soda water

MAMA SAYS...

History provides clues to the origins of this dish. South Africa was settled from the seventeenth century onwards by colonists who brought European cookery styles with them. The French, known for making wines, began establishing vineyards, Germans introduced baked goods and pastries, and the British brought meat pies.

Curry Goat

The seductive spiciness of this dish is testament to the Malay influence on South African cuisine, most notable in the form of curries, chilies and extensive use of spices such as ginger, cinnamon and turmeric.

Place oil in large pot. Add garlic, onion and ginger sauté until onion is translucent. Add the goat meat and cook until light brown on all sides. Add all the spices, sugar and salt stir just a few more minutes. Add water and tomatoes simmered for 2 hours. Add the potatoes and simmer for an additional hour. Add cilantro and serve.

Makes 6 servings.

1/4 cup olive oil

3 cloves garlic chopped

1-1/2 onions, sliced ½ inch thin

1-1/2 tablespoons fresh ginger, peeled and chopped

5 pounds of goat meat, stew cut (on the bone)

1 tablespoon ground cumin

1 tablespoon ground coriander

2 cinnamon sticks

1 tablespoon cardamom seeds

1 tablespoon whole cloves

1 tablespoon turmeric

1 tablespoon chili powder

1 tablespoon salt

2 tablespoons sugar

4 cups water

3 potatoes, peeled and cubed

2 cups tomatoes, chopped

1/2 bunch fresh cilantro, crushed

MAMA SAYS...

When a local farmer introduced me to his goat meat, it reminded me of our South African Boer goats, and the Malaysian-inspired dishes of my homeland. The taste of goat meat is similar to that of lamb, and, for that matter, this recipe will work as well with practically any stew meat. For culinary authenticity, serve with basmati rice (recipe p. 82), dried fruit chutney (recipe p. 46), and Malay roti (recipe p. 36), sliced bananas, and shredded coconut. I like to set it all up on a buffet table and let people add their own toppings.

Desserts

"Simply" Red Velvet Cake

Red cake? You've got to be kidding! That was my reaction when a waiter I worked with in Boston introduced me to this recipe. But my affinity for the color attracted me to this regional favorite. It's a "simple" but wonderful treat on a hot summer's day after some smoky barbeque. Red Velvet Cake originated in the South in the early 1900s; at first, beets provided the dramatic color. It is beautifully textured, and cocoa adds chocolate notes to the flavors. Thick, very white cream cheese icing masks the red color before the cake is cut, then provides contrast.

For the cake:
- 1/2 cup butter, room temp.
- 1-1/2 cup white sugar
- 1 teaspoon vanilla
- 2-1/2 cups white flour
- 1 teaspoon baking powder
- 1/2 teaspoon salt
- 2 tablespoons cocoa
- 1 cup buttermilk
- 2 tablespoons red food coloring
- 2 eggs
- 1 teaspoon white vinegar
- 1 teaspoon baking soda

For the frosting:
- 8 ounces cream cheese at room temperature
- 1 pound powdered sugar
- 2 cups shredded coconut (toasted in a 350-degree oven for 7 minutes)

For the cake: place the butter, sugar and vanilla in the mixer and mix with the paddle attachment until creamy white. Sift the flour, baking powder, salt and cocoa together add slowly to the butter mixture. Whisk the red food coloring and buttermilk together and add slowly to the mix. Mix the white vinegar and baking soda together and add to the mix until just combined. Scrape into two 9-inch cake pans coated with non-stick spray. Bake on the center rack of a a pre-heated oven for 20 to 25 minutes at 350-degrees, until an inserted toothpick will come out clean. Allow to cool.

For the frosting: place the cream cheese in the mixer with a whip attachment and turn it on. Slowly add the powdered sugar and whip until light and creamy. To frost the cake, use a table knife and a glass of very hot water (hot water makes spreading easier and cleans the knife between each spread). Frost the first layer, add the second layer. Frost the second layer, then around the sides of the cake. Press the toasted coconut around the sides and top.

MAMA SAYS...

Some of you may know Red Velvet as the "Armadillo Cake" from the movie Steel Magnolias.

Shoofly Pie

Perhaps no other single dessert is so identified with the Pennsylvania Dutch as is shoofly pie. The gooey, mouth-watering pie depends on dark, backstrap molasses for its deep, distinctive flavor. Best served at room temperature with dollops of whipped cream.

For the crust: in a food processor place the flour, salt, sugar and butter. Pulse until it reaches a crumble form. Add in the egg yolk and water. Continue to pulse just until the mix comes together. Press into a 9 inch pie tin (with a removable bottom).

For the filling: in a large bowl, using two knives, cut the butter, sugar, flour and salt in together until crumbles are the size of small peas. In a large bowl, whisk together the baking soda and water. Add the molasses, corn syrup and egg and continue to whisk. When thoroughly combined, pour into prepared shell, filling to half. (Do not overfill the shell or it will overflow during baking). Gently sprinkle the prepared crumb mixture evenly over the top of the pie some of the crumbs will sink to the bottom. Bake in a pre-heated oven at 400-degrees for 10 minutes, then reduce to 350-degrees and bake an additional 35-40 minutes, until an inserted knife will come out clean. Remove from oven and cool on a wire rack. Top with whipped cream, slice and serve.

Makes 8 servings.

For the crust:

2 cups flour

Pinch salt

4-1/2 tablespoons white granulated sugar

15 tablespoons unsalted butter

2 egg yolks

1/2 tablespoon cold water

For the filling:

3 tablespoons unsalted butter, room temperature

1-1/2 cups flour

2/3 cups brown sugar, firmly packed

pinch of salt

1 teaspoon baking soda

1 cup hot water

1/2 cup black strap molasses

1/2 cup corn syrup

1 egg

MAMA SAYS...

I've always been intrigued by the name. The most logical explanation is related to the fact that in years past, when pies were placed on window sills to cool, housewives constantly had to "shoo" away flies from the sweet, sticky pies.

Lemon Pound Cake with Lemon Curd

It's a moist, finely-textured, sweet (but not too sweet), and refreshingly tart cake, intended to accompany a pot of tea, in the civilized Southern tradition. With lemon-flavored cake and homemade lemon curd, you won't find a more lemony recipe than this. It can be garnished with sliced fruits like blueberries and strawberries and topped with fresh whipped cream. It's great to enjoy in the middle of summer when local fruits are at their peak or in the winter with canned fruit from the previous season. Even the thinnest slice is satisfying.

For the lemon curd: in a heavy bottom sauce pan place the lemon juice, eggs and sugar. On medium heat whisk the mixture until it is thick and bubbling. Whisk in the butter. Remove from heat and allow to cool. Place a piece of plastic wrap directly onto the curd so that no film forms on the curd. Refrigerate until ready to use.

For the pound cake: preheat oven to 325-degrees. Butter and flour a 9x5x2 metal loaf pan. Sift flour, baking powder and salt. Using a stand mixer beat the sugar and butter until well blended. Add in the eggs one at a time, then the buttermilk, lemon zest and lemon juice. Pour the batter into the pan. Sprinkle the top with the remaining sugar. Bake for 45 to 55 minutes. (Test the cake for doneness with a cake tester or wooden pick. Insert it into the center of the cake. It should come out clean with no batter clinging to it). Allow to cool. Cut into slices and top with lemon curd, fruits, and fresh whipped cream.

For the lemon curd:
3/4 cups lemon juice
4 eggs
12 ounces granulated white sugar
6 ounces unsalted butter

For the pound cake:
1-1/2 cups sifted flour
1/2 tablespoons baking powder
pinch of salt
1-3/4 cups granulated white sugar
1-1/2 sticks butter
3 eggs
1/2 cup buttermilk
Zest of 1 lemon
3 tablespoons lemon juice

Makes 6 servings.

It's important to have the butter and eggs at room temperature so the maximum amount of air can be beaten into the batter.

MAMA SAYS...

Thanksgiving Pecan Pie

Soon after settling in New Orleans, the French were introduced to the rich, buttery pecan by Native Americans. They promptly made good use of it by creating pecan brittle, pecan pralines, pecan sauce, and, of course, pecan pie. The dessert has become a traditional Thanksgiving dessert, but I think of it as home-cooked comfort food, good any old time. This is an adaptation of a recipe that I found in Louisiana, using cane syrup instead of corn syrup and toasting the nuts before adding them to the mix for a nuttier, fuller flavor in the pie.

For the pie crust:
- 2 cups white flour
- pinch of salt
- 4 tablespoons granulated white sugar
- 15 tablespoons unsalted butter cut into cubes
- 2 eggs
- 2 tablespoons ice cold water

For the filling:
- 1 cup pecans, coated with butter
- 3 eggs
- 3/4 cup granulated white sugar
- 3/4 cup Steen's cane syrup
- 1/4 cup molasses
- pinch salt
- 2 tablespoon butter, melted
- 1 teaspoon vanilla

For the pie crust: place all ingredients except the water in mixer with a blade attachment. Pulse the mix until crumbly. Add the water and continue to pulse until it begins to come together. Divide the dough between six 3-1/2-inch pie tins with removable bottoms. Use your thumb to press the dough up the sides of the tin distributing the dough evenly. Place tins onto a cookie sheet tray and set aside until the filling is ready.

For the filling: spread out the butter-coated pecans on a non-stick cookie sheet in a single layer. Toast in a pre-heated oven for 5 to 6 minutes at 400-degrees, until crisp and aromatic. Allow to cool. Whisk all ingredients together until well combined. Ladle filling into the pie tins, distributing the filling evenly. Place in a pre-heated oven and bake at 400-degrees for 15 minutes. Reduce temperature to 350-degrees and bake an additional 15 minutes. (Filling will puff and crack slightly when done). Cool slightly. Remove the pie from the tin. Serve with whipped cream or ice cream.

Makes 6 servings.

MAMA SAYS...

You can make them as individual pies but this recipe also works for a 9-inch pie tin.

Chocolate Whiskey Pudding

There is something very elegant and Southern about bourbon, the grand old whiskey of Bourbon County, Kentucky. In its harmonious partnership with chocolate, bourbon adds a strong dose of booze to a glorified bread pudding, an honored confection of the South. Served warm, the cake foundation nicely sops up the sweet sauce, and each lovin' spoonful is filled with a synergy of flavors at play.

For the sauce: whisk all ingredients together in a small sauce pan. Heat on low until all the sugar has melted and the sauce is warm.

For the cake: butter an 8x8-inch cake pan. In a stand mixer with paddle attachment, beat the sugar and butter on low. Add the flour, cocoa powder, baking powder and salt and continue to mix. Add in the buttermilk, bourbon, vanilla, and pecans. Once the mix has come together in the bowl, turn off and scrape down the sides into the cake pan. Pour the sauce over the batter. Place in a preheated oven and bake for 35 minutes at 350-degrees. Remove from the oven, cool slightly, and serve while still warm (can be kept in the oven on 200-degrees until you are ready to serve).

For the whipped cream: beat in a stand mixer with the whip attachment until stiff peaks form.

Makes 6 servings.

For the sauce:
3/4 cup packed light brown sugar
1/4 cup sweetened cocoa powder
1-1/3 cup water
1/3 cup bourbon
1-1/3 teaspoons vanilla
1/8 teaspoon salt

For the cake:
3 tablespoons butter (plus extra to butter the pan)
3/4 cup white sugar
1 cup sifted flour
1/4 cup unsweetened cocoa powder
2 teaspoons baking powder
1/2 teaspoon salt
1 cup toasted pecans, coarsely chopped
1/3 cup buttermilk
1-1/2 tsp bourbon
1/2 tsp vanilla

For the whipped cream:
1 cup heavy whipping cream
2 tablespoons granulated sugar
2 tablespoons bourbon

MAMA SAYS...

Dessert is the last thing my guests taste before they leave the restaurant, so I want to make sure it rocks. This dish delights everyone.

Beignets

In New Orleans, "coffee and doughnuts" means strong, chicory-laced café au lait and beignets (pronounced "ben-YAY"). These crispy, chewy fritters (introduced in the 1800s by the French Acadians) have become the toast of the town. Proper beignets are always dusted with a thick blanket of powdered sugar.

Heat milk, butter, water and salt until the butter is just melted. Add the flour and continue to cook on low for two more minutes. Pull off the heat and allow to cool for 5 minutes. Scrape into a stand mixer, then add the eggs one at a time. Heat oil in a heavy bottom one-gallon pot (use a pot that is twice the volume of the oil). Use a candy thermometer to monitor the temperature of the oil at 350-degrees. Once the oil has reached temperature, drop tablespoon-sized portions of dough into the oil, using a second tablespoon to push the dough off the spoon (work in batches of 6 at a time). Fry for 10 minutes, until they float to the top, then use a pair of tongs to pull them out of the oil. The beignets can be kept warm in a 250-degree oven until all batches have been fried. After removing from the oil, place the powdered sugar into a sieve and generously dust the beignets with the sugar.

1/2 cup whole milk

6 tablespoons unsalted butter

1/2 cup water

1/2 teaspoons salt

1 cup flour

4 eggs

4 cups vegetable oil for frying

Makes 12 servings.

After frying them up, let the kids take turns shaking the beignets in a paper bag with powdered sugar. The sugar will end up all over their faces, but that's part of the fun.

Praline Pecans

The original French praline was named after 17th-century diplomat Cesar Duplessis-Praslin, who is said to have shared his chef's sugary almond confections with Louis XIII. When New Orleans was settled by French colonists, native pecans were substituted for the almonds and the sugar brittle was made with Louisiana sugar cane. Pralines are best when consumed immediately and will stay good for up to two weeks. Due to the crystallization of the sugar, the texture does change to a harder, more sugary confection after several days.

1 cup white granulated sugar

1/2 cup dark brown sugar packed

2 pinches salt

1/2 cup half and half

1 cup chopped toasted pecans

1 tablespoon butter

1 teaspoon vanilla

Place the white sugar, brown sugar, salt and half and half in a heavy bottom saucepan over medium heat. Stir with a wooden spoon until the sugar has melted. Add in the pecans and butter and continue to stir (monitor with a candy thermometer until it reaches 230-degrees). Turn off the heat and pour in the vanilla. Continue to stir for 4-8 minutes, until the candy has thickened considerably. Pour the candy, one tablespoon at a time, onto a wax sheet of paper on a cookie sheet and allow to cool for 10 minutes. Store in an air-tight container.

MAMA SAYS...

In New Orleans, the local and proper pronunciation is "prah-lean," while the nut in it is pronounced "peck-on."

Blackberry & Peach Cobbler

The search for happiness through food is successfully demonstrated by this Southern deep-dish favorite, a tradition at picnics and family gatherings. My cobbler recipe beautifully combines the flavors and colors of two fruits you might not think of pairing together, best made and served in the height of the local fruit season.

For the filling:

Toss the blackberries and peaches with sugar and allow to stand 30 minutes, tossing frequently. Drain the fruit. Whisk together the sugar, cornstarch, lemon juice and salt and add to the fruit. Place the fruit in a 9-inch baking dish and bake in a 350-degree oven for 10 minutes. Remove from the oven and top with the cobbler topping.

For the topping:

In a food processor, combine the flour, cornmeal, white sugar, baking powder, baking soda, salt and butter. Pulse until the mix resembles a coarse meal.

Place into a mixing bowl and add the lemon zest and the buttermilk. Top the fruit with the cobbler mix. Return to the oven and bake for an additional 15 minutes, until golden brown and bubbly.

Makes 6 servings.

For the filling:
1 pound blackberries
1 pound peaches, sliced
1/4 cup granulated white sugar
1 teaspoon cornstarch
1 tablespoon lemon juice
zest of 1 lemon
pinch salt

For the topping:
1-1/2 cups flour
1/2 cup cornmeal
6 tablespoons plus 2 teaspoons
**   granulated white sugar**
1-1/2 teaspoons baking powder
1/2 teaspoon baking soda
1/2 teaspoon salt
10 tablespoons butter
2/3 cups buttermilk
zest of 2 lemons

MAMA SAYS...

The fruit part of this cobbler can be traded out with other ingredients in season. Try fresh strawberries and rhubarb.

Slow-Ass Spiced & Spiked Apple Cake

An array of autumn spices tickle the taste buds in this rustic apple cake, best baked during local apple harvest. I like to jack up the spices with the rich flavors of dark rum. Serve warm, piled with fresh whipped cream.

For the cake batter: mix all the dry ingredients together and then add in the raisins and apples. Whisk together all wet ingredients, then add to the dry ingredients and combine. Scrape the batter into a 9-inch-square baking pan (sprayed with non-stick spray) and bake in a pre-heated oven for 45 minutes at 375-degrees.

For the caramel sauce: place the sugar in a heavy bottom pot on medium heat, and continuously stir with a wooden spoon (the sugar will slowly begin to melt and caramelize once all the sugar has melted). Pour in 2 cups of the heavy cream very slowly (it will sputter and boil up a little it may even clump, have no fear, turn down the heat to low, stir occasionally as the cream comes to temperature). Add in the cinnamon and apple cider and simmer for about 15 minutes. Allow to cool, then pour into a sealed container. (The caramel sauce and apple cider will separate slightly while being stored; just stir it up every time you use it).

To serve: slice the cake into 6 servings. Place into bowls and top each serving with 1/3 cup caramel sauce. Whip remaining 1 cup of heavy cream to soft peaks and top each dessert. Sprinkle a mix of cinnamon and brown sugar to finish.

Makes 6 servings.

For the cake batter:

- 1 cup cornmeal
- 1 cup flour
- 1-1/2 tablespoons cinnamon
- 1-1/2 tablespoons ground allspice
- 1-1/2 tablespoons ground ginger
- 1 tablespoon ground clove
- 1/2 tablespoon salt
- 1/2 tablespoon baking powder
- 1/2 tablespoon baking soda
- 1/2 cup raisins
- 2 apples, cut into chunks, skin on
- 1/2 cup vegetable oil
- 1/4 cup granulated white sugar
- 1 egg
- 1/4 cup backstrap molasses
- 1/4 cup dark rum
- 1/4 cup maple syrup

For the caramel sauce:

- 1/2 pound white granulated sugar
- 3 cups heavy cream
- 1 cinnamon stick
- 1/4 cup fresh apple cider or apple juice

MAMA SAYS...

Inspired by the jar of "Slow Ass" brand backstrap molasses I found in a Florida grocery store, I couldn't resist keeping the name (and the ingredient) as I developed my recipe for this apple cake. Don't be shy – when you order it in the restaurant, ask for it by its full name.

Melk Tert

A much-loved Dutch recipe traditionally served in South African homes with tea, and, as you may have already guessed, it translates to "milk tart." The light, delicate custard provides the perfect accompaniment to a fragrant pot of herbal rooibos tea. It's absolutely delicious if you eat it warm, just as it's made.

For the pie crust: Pulse the sugar, salt, butter and cream cheese in a food processor until well combined. Add the flour and mix until the dough comes together. Press the dough into 6 individual 3-1/2 inch deep pie tins with removable bottoms. Chill the dough in the pie tins for 1 hour. In a preheated oven, bake the empty pie shells for 15 minutes at 350-degrees. Remove from the oven and fill each pie tin with 4 ounces of filling. Return to the oven and bake for an additional 5 minutes. Remove from the oven and allow to cool. Sprinkle the top with the cinnamon and sugar mixture.

For the filling: in a small saucepan whisk together the flour, cornstarch and white sugar. In small increments, add the milk. When all milk has been incorporated, add in the cinnamon sticks and cardamom seeds. Place the milk on the stove on medium heat and simmer until the milk has thickened noticeably. Remove from heat, then whisk in the butter, vanilla and three yolks. Beat the egg whites until stiff and then fold it into the custard. Fill the pie tins.

Makes 6 servings.

For the pie crust:
2 tablespoons granulated white sugar

1/4 teaspoon salt

1 stick of butter

1-1/4 cups flour

2 ounces cream cheese

1 tablespoon cinnamon

1 tablespoon brown sugar

For the filling:
1-1/2 ounces flour

3 tablespoons cornstarch

4 ounces granulated white sugar

3 eggs, separated

2-1/4 cups milk

1 cinnamon stick

3 cardamom seeds

1/2 ounce butter

1 teaspoon vanilla

MAMA SAYS...

Rooibos tea (pronounced "roy-boss") should be steeped with boiling water for at least 5 minutes to release its full flavors.

About the Band

The Evil City String Band grew out of a vibrant

old-time Appalachian music scene that exists in and around the Finger Lakes region of New York.

More specifically, Ithaca and Trumansburg, New York have been home to a large number of musicians who play traditional, as well as original music. Also a tradition in these parts is the combination of great food, great wine, and great music enjoyed simultaneously in a casual, family-oriented, communal atmosphere. This combination has become a renowned part of the local culture, and people come from miles around to enjoy and partake.

Samantha Izzo's Simply Red Bistro and The Evil City String Band came together in Trumansburg when Sam and I, the band's leader, Richie Stearn, joined forces with their particular talents to further the communal tradition.

I sing and song-write, plus play banjo, as well as organize sessions of local and nationally touring bands to play many local establishments. My band includes Steve Selin on fiddle, Paddy Burke on guitar, and Ben Gould on doghouse bass. Sam's fiery and feisty, and passionate ways about her food, and about creating a new scene in a tired world appealed to us. We started by simply showing up to play every week for the past five years, with the ulterior motive of eating Sam's fried chicken and collared greens, and drinking free locally produced wines!

Nothing makes you sing better than a belly full of good food.

Old time Appalachian music is not pretentious, not even performance oriented; it's people's music. It's music to dance to, eat to, drink to, and talk over. It creates an atmosphere of celebration of the basic good things in life by expressing the hard times as well as the good times.

To the players, it is trance-like music, highly repetitive and rhythmic, with often haunting lyrics loosely thrown over the tune like a battered jacket on a cold day. We are very proud to hand over our music to Sam to help her promote her new cookbook, and that's why we recorded the accompanying CD.

Richie Stearns
Bandleader

Recipe Index

Beverages

Hot Cocoa with Ginger-Chipotle Cream - page 15

Iced Coffee with Steen's - page 10

Mint Julep - page 13

Porch Swing Cocktail - page 12

Sangaree - page 14

"Simply" Red Tea - page 9

Soda Fountain Lemonade - page 11

Beef

Blue Plate Special Meatloaf - page 90

Chicken-Fried Steak and Vidalia Onion Gravy - page 96

Breads

Cracked Wheat Rolls - page 34

"Dead Banana" Bread - page 31

Double-Corn & Zucchini Spoon Bread - page 32

Down-Home Buttermilk Biscuits - page 30

Drop Biscuits with Cheddar & Black Pepper - page 29

Hushpuppies - page 33

Kickass Cornbread - page 27

Malay Roti - page 36

Rustic Flatbread - page 28

VetKoek - page 35

Chicken

Chicken Livers Peri-Peri - page 70

Fearless Lemon-Garlic-Red Pepper Chicken - page 103

Grandma Willie's Chicken Pie - page 104

Honey-Stung Fried Chicken - page 87

Honest-to-Goodness Chicken Pot Pie - page 95

Dessert

Beignets - page 114

Blackberry & Peach Cobbler - page 116

Chocolate Whiskey Pudding - page 113

Lemon Pound Cake with Lemon Curd - page 111

Milk Tert - page 118

Praline Pecans - page 115

Shoofly Pie - page 110

"Simply" Red Velvet Cake - page 109

Slow-Ass Spiced & Spiked Apple Cake - page 117

Thanksgiving Pecan Pie - page 112

Goat

Curry Goat - page 105

Pork

Best Damn Barbeque Ribs - page 89

Family Reunion Dinner Ham - page 88

Salads

BLT Iceberg Wedge - page 10

Caesar Salad - page 53

Caesar Salad Supreme - page 54

Glorified Potato Eater's Salad - page 52

Kicked-Up Coleslaw - page 49

Watermelon Summer Salad - page 55

Sauces, Dressings and Butters

Angry Vinegar - page 56

Best Damn Barbeque Sauce - page 43

Cajun Butter - page 80

Cajun Remoulade - page 39

Creamy Blue Cheese Dressing - page 11

Curry Mayonnaise - page 40

Dried Fruit Chutney - page 46

Garlic Herb Butter - page 45

Honey Butter - page 44

Orange-Chipotle Vinaigrette - page 42

Roasted Garlic-Lemon Aioli - page 41

Seafood - Soup

Shrimp Bisque - page 68
with Crème Fraiche and Shitake Mushrooms

Seafood = Appetizer

Hot Dixie Dip = page 69

Seafood = Main Dish

Boardwalk Crab Cakes = page 94
with Lemon=Caper=Garlic Aioli

Cajun Cornmeal=Crusted Catfish = page 91

Creole Jambalaya = page 92

Killer Shrimp = page 99

True Shrimp and Grits = page 93

Vegetables = Main Course

Mac-and-Cheese Deluxe = page 100

Veggie Cheeseburger with Barbeque Sauce = page 101

"Where's the Beef" Chili = page 102

Vegetables = Soup

Sweet Potato=Roasted Red Pepper=Butternut Soup = page 67

with Chipotle Pepper Cream

Vegetables - Side Dish

Buttermilk Mashed Potatoes - page 73

Collard Greens with Ham Hock - page 51

Fragrant Basmati Rice - page 52

Fried Green Tomatoes - page 63

Garlic and Herb Fries - page 66

Homestyle Potato Chips - page 65

Hoppin' John - page 78

Okra and Tomatoes - page 76

Roasted Root Vegetables - page 79

Saturday Morning Supper Hash - page 74

Sweet Corn on the Cob - page 77

T-Burg Sweet-Potato Fries - page 64

Truck-Stop Barbeque Beans - page 75

Wild Rice - page 53

Measurement Conversion Tables

Measurement Conversion Tables

Metric to U.S.: Capacity

1 militers = 1/5 teaspoon

5 ml = 1 teaspoon

15 ml = 1 tablespoon

30 ml = 1 fluid oz.

100 ml = 3.4 fluid oz.

240 ml = 1 cup

1 liter = 34 fluid oz.

1 liter = 4.2 cups

1 liter = 2.1 pints

1 liter = 1.06 quarts

1 liter = .26 gallon

U.S. to Metric: Capacity

1/5 teaspoon = 1 ml

1 teaspoon = 5 ml

1 tablespoon = 15 ml

1 fluid oz. = 30 ml

1/5 cup = 50 ml

1 cup = 240 ml

2 cups (1 pint) = 470 ml

4 cups (1 quart) = .95 liter

4 quarts (1 gal.) = 3.8 liters

Metric to U.S.: Capacity

1 gram = .035 ounce

100 grams = 3.5 ounces

500 grams = 1.10 pounds

1 kilogram = 2.205 pounds

1 kilogram = 35 oz.

U.S. to Metric: Weight

1 oz. = 28 grams

1 pound = 454 grams

Cooking Measurement Equivalents

16 tablespoons = 1 cup

12 tablespoons = 3/4 cup

10 tablespoons + 2 teaspoons = 2/3 cup

8 tablespoons = 1/2 cup

6 tablespoons = 3/8 cup

5 tablespoons + 1 teaspoon = 1/3 cup

4 tablespoons = 1/4 cup

2 tablespoons = 1/8 cup

2 tablespoons + 2 teaspoons = 1/6 cup

1 tablespoon = 1/16 cup

2 cups = 1 pint

2 pints = 1 quart

3 teaspoons = 1 tablespoon

48 teaspoons = 1 cup

SIDE ORDER BOOKS
www.sideorderbooks.com

We assist restaurants and wineries
in the development, publishing, and promotion
of creative book projects.

For more information, email:
sideorderbooks@gmail.com

Or, visit the website:
www.sideorderbooks.com

LAKESIDE BISTRO
AT SHELDRAKE POINT

7448 County Road 153
Ovid, New York 14521

Simply Red Bistro at Sheldrake Point Vineyard is located on the western shore of Cayuga Lake, in the heart of New York's scenic Finger Lakes Region, just 20 miles north of Ithaca and 20 miles south of Geneva/Seneca Falls.

Mama Red's Comfort Kitchen
makes a great gift!

To order additional copies for others who might also enjoy this book,

or

to order the companion CD of music:

Monday Nights at Simply Red Bistro
(by The Evil City String Band)

go to:

www.simplyredbistro.com